10

Traits of Highly Effective Teachers

To Emily McEwan-Fujita
and
Patrick J. McEwan

10 Traits of Highly Effective Teachers

How to Hire, Coach, and Mentor Successful Teachers

Elaine K. McEwan

CORWIN PRESS, INC.
A Sage Publications Company
Thousand Oaks, California

For information:

Corwin Press, Inc.
A Sage Publications Company
2455 Teller Road
Thousand Oaks, California 91320
E-mail: order@corwinpress.com

Sage Publications Ltd.
6 Bonhill Street
London EC2A 4PU
United Kingdom

Sage Publications India Pvt. Ltd.
M-32 Market
Greater Kailash I
New Delhi 110 048 India

Printed in the United States of America

Library of Congress Cataloging-in-Publication Data

McEwan, Elaine K., 1941-
    Ten traits of highly effective teachers: How to hire, coach, and mentor successful teachers / by Elaine K. McEwan.
        p. cm.
    Includes bibliographical references and index.
    ISBN 0-7619-7783-X (c) — ISBN 0-7619-7784-8 (p)
    1. Effective teaching. 2. Mentoring in education. 3. Educational leadership.   I. Title.
    LB1025.3 .M355 2001
    371.102—dc21   2001002419

This book is printed on acid-free paper.

06 07 08 09 10 11 10 9 8 7 6

Acquiring Editor:	Robb Clouse
Associate Editor:	Kylee Liegl
Corwin Editorial Assistant:	Erin Buchanan
Production Editor:	Diane S. Foster
Editorial Assistant:	Cindy Bear
Copy Editor:	Rachel Hile Bassett
Typesetter:	Marion Warren
Proofreader:	Scott Oney
Cover Designer:	Michael Dubowe

Contents

Preface

The success of a school depends, in large measure, on the quality of its teaching staff. When teachers are effective, students learn. When teachers are skilled, parents are happy. When teachers look good, their principals also look good. However, what does an effective teacher actually look like? What are the traits that characterize skillful and successful teachers?

Those of us with years of administrative experience have discovered that identifying these paragons of pedagogical virtue based on a short interview or a written application is a formidable task. Transcripts and recommendations are only as good as the universities and individuals that issue them. Appearances are sometimes deceiving. Administrators (myself included) can be the victims of our own prejudices or personalities—hiring graduates of our alma maters or eliminating candidates who fail to laugh at our jokes. Sometimes we're like last-minute holiday shoppers—frantic to make a decision and cross one more vacancy off our list. Or, we may not have a clear picture of just what to look for in a teacher. We're unaware of the important characteristics of a successful teacher—those traits that are essential no matter what the size, shape, age, gender, or fashion preferences of the individual may be. We are, in fact, often distracted by irrelevant variables, forgetting that the ten traits of highly effective teachers are packaged in an infinite number of ways.

Hiring new staff members is not the only time that administrators need to know what a good teacher looks like. Few of us have had the privilege of handpicking a complete teaching staff. More often, we're stuck with someone else's choices and are faced with supervision, evaluation, and even remediation. I recently conducted a workshop titled *Improving Reading Instruction in Grades K–2*. The majority of participants, elementary school principals, watched a videotaped reading lesson and jotted down their answers to the following questions:

- What behaviors of the teacher were effective and should be continued in further lessons?

- What behaviors of the teacher were ineffective and should be eliminated or minimized in further lessons?

- What effective teaching behaviors that were missing from the lesson should be initiated/included in subsequent lessons?

At the conclusion of the viewing and note taking, the principals gathered in small groups to discuss and summarize their findings. The conversations were animated, and, not surprisingly, the participants had strong and varied opinions about the teacher's effectiveness.

Some principals were effusive in their praise of the videotaped teacher. "She's terrific. I'd hire her in a heartbeat," said one principal.

"She definitely needs some coaching," suggested another. "But she's certainly better than most of the candidates I've seen lately."

"I have real reservations about her based on *this* lesson," opined another. "If I can't figure out what she's talking about, how can a group of first-graders?"

Others didn't like what she was wearing and how she sat. "Unprofessional!"

The brand-new administrators in the group listened in astonishment to the lively exchange. They were hoping for answers. Instead, they got ambiguity. "Just what *should* I be looking for during an observation?" said one in desperation. The few teacher participants in attendance were grateful that *they* were not being dissected and discussed by these picky principals.

In an *Education Week* essay on teacher preparation, Richard Andrews related a conversation he held with the oldest living schoolteacher in the United States. This outspoken senior citizen didn't mince any words on the subject of teacher quality. "Since I can remember, there have always been three kinds of teachers," she said. "One group was just born to teach. A second group was born and should not teach. A third group should never have been born at all" (2000, p. 37). You might be able to chuckle at this blunt assessment if you haven't personally experienced the second and third groups up close. Those of us who have (the writer included) aren't laughing—we're crying. We know from our own experiences that poor teachers add stress and sleepless nights to principals' lives, contribute to low staff morale, and create scores of angry parents. However, most depressing of all is that ineffective teachers damage students and diminish learning (Sanders & Rivers, 1996).

Administrators aren't the only ones who need to know what a good teacher looks like. Brand-new and even experienced teachers are eager to find out just what constitutes a highly effective teacher and how they can become one. Many are feeling as beleaguered as their principals. "Raise test scores. Meet the needs of the gifted. Teach included children. *And,* don't forget to leap tall buildings in a single bound." One teacher summarized the pressures: "[We] are asked to be the writer and performer in a different five-hour play every day. It's not easy for us to tailor and perform one effective five-hour script a day, much less different scripts for the middle, top and bottom" (Nelson, 2000, p. A22). How can one individual do all of this? By being a highly effective teacher.

The Origin of the Ten Traits

You may be curious about the origin of the ten traits I have chosen to include in this book. I have read widely in the literature (descriptive, qualitative, and quantitative) regarding the traits of effective teachers. I paid particular attention to the research that illuminates the relationship between what teachers do while they are teaching and how well their students achieve—an area of critical concern in today's era of accountability. I then submitted my list of traits to a variety of outstanding educators and asked them to consider the priority of each one for inclusion in the final list. I also asked them to reflect on how these traits found expression in their personal teaching lives. They wrote essays, made lists, told stories, and even sent me copies of their published work. Their reflections and observations are included throughout the book. I also listened to what students had to say about the traits that are important to them in a teacher, and you will find some of their opinions and ideas in the book as well.

In addition to consulting the experts, I have also written about what I know personally, and I have known a lot of teachers in my lifetime. First, I am a teacher myself. I began my career as a teacher and I have returned to teaching—teaching educators all over the country, several thousand of them over the past 3 years. My sister is a teacher, both of my children teach at the college level, and even my favorite next-door neighbor is a teacher. During my several careers as a student, teacher, librarian, principal, central office administrator, and parent of two children, I've encountered and worked with hundreds of teachers. I've hired them, mentored them, motivated them, coached them, and in some difficult cases, I've terminated them.

Who This Book Is For

This book is designed for educators on both sides of the desk—administrators and teachers. I have written *Ten Traits of Highly Effective Teachers* for results-oriented administrators who daily face the pressures of accountability. Engaged and high-achieving students, whether 5-year-olds or freshmen, don't just happen. They blossom under the tutelage of skillful teachers. The ability to recognize and nurture effective teachers is an essential skill of the instructional leader. Principals, human resource administrators, and superintendents will find ideas and information in this book that will (a) help them improve instruction in their schools; (b) inspire them to become more able mentors and coaches to their teachers; and (c) assist them in making decisions about teaching personnel. Trainers of teachers will also find this book to be useful as they work with students in preservice preparation. My selection of traits and the suggested interview questions that accompany each one will engender many lively discussions.

I have written this book for teachers as well—not only for newcomers who are looking for information and inspiration as they seek to write their own personal definitions of highly effective teaching, but also for experienced teachers who need affirmation and validation that the calling they once felt to teach is still alive and well.

This book will not only increase administrators' abilities to hire, coach, mentor, and motivate effective teachers, it will also give every teacher, whether a beginner or a master, a renewed sense of mission and vision for what teaching can be.

Overview of the Contents

Chapter 1 describes a variety of memorable teachers, gives a brief historical overview of the search for a definition of the "effective" teacher, and then introduces you to each of the 10 traits through brief vignettes and first-person reflections. You will discover that the ten traits fall into three distinct categories:

1. *Personal* traits that signify character

2. *Teaching* traits that get results

3. *Intellectual* traits that demonstrate knowledge, curiosity, and awareness

Just who *is* the effective teacher? The "big picture" will emerge once you have finished reading Chapter 1.

Chapters 2 through 6 describe the 10 traits in more detail—fleshing out the critical attributes of each one and providing research, where applicable, that links the traits to student achievement. In addition to the narrative descriptions, you will also find numerous graphic organizers to help you to preview the traits before you read about them or to refresh your memory after reading.

Chapter 2 details the personal traits that signify character: (1) Mission-Driven and Passionate; (2) Positive and Real; and (3) A Teacher-Leader. When adults are asked to talk about teachers who made a difference in their lives, they will inevitably describe these individuals in terms of personal traits—words like "warm, caring, tough as nails, demanding," or other descriptive words that denote human characteristics (Koehn, 1984, p. 162). In Chapter 2, the "human" traits receive top billing.

Chapters 3, 4, and 5 describe the teaching traits that get results. Chapter 3 describes (4) With-it-ness and (5) Style. Chapter 4 explains the complexities of (6) Motivational Expertise, and Chapter 5 completes the presentation of the teaching traits with (7) Instructional Effectiveness— the essence of the teaching process. The highly effective teacher can skillfully organize a classroom, design a compelling lesson that incorporates just what learners need, and then convince even the most reluctant students that they *can* learn and that this teacher is just the person to get the job done. The effective teacher gets results. "There is more to good teaching than skill, but there's no good teaching without it" (Saphier & Gower, 1967, p. 3).

Chapter 6 describes the intellectual traits that indicate knowledge, curiosity, and awareness: (8) Book Learning; (9) Street Smarts; and (10) A Mental Life. Teachers who do not possess knowledge, curiosity, and awareness are like a beautiful goblet that is empty. "A teacher must seek to have a full command of a subject. . . . A teacher should know enough to be a thinker as well as an instructor" (Banner & Cannon, 1997, p. 11).

Chapter 7 describes the hiring process. I have assembled a panel of experienced administrators to advise you. Listen in while they talk about how they interview and select teachers. The induction, orientation, and mentoring processes are featured in Chapter 8—how new teachers and teachers new to a school can be supported and encouraged in their efforts to become effective. There are more than 30 things that principals can do for and with new teachers to help them feel included and be successful as well as ways to encourage experienced teachers to support their new colleagues. Finally, Chapter 9 gives suggestions regarding how experienced teachers can be empowered and energized—through personal reflection and study, staff development activities, and administrative instructional leadership. If your teachers need to have their batteries recharged, you will find something to please everyone on your staff in the 24 activities designed to motivate experienced teachers. There are also several helpful resources at the conclusion of the book. Don't overlook them. You will find the following:

- A full set of all the graphic organizers that are included throughout the book

- A complete list of the 10 traits with their descriptions for quick reference

- A collection of more than 50 interview questions, several for each trait—useful for administrators who are interviewing teacher candidates, for trainers of teachers for in-class discussion and role-playing, and for teachers prepping for an all-important interview

- A set of recommended readings especially chosen to deepen your understanding and appreciation of each trait

- A set of reflective exercises for each trait that can be used by individual teachers or small study groups

Acknowledgments

This book would not have been possible without the contributions of many highly effective educators—teachers, principals, central office administrators, and university professors. They answered my questions, returned my phone calls, responded to my e-mails, and sent me supporting documents and information. They will speak to you throughout the book, but I want to thank them personally here. Marsha Arest is my next-door neighbor, if only for a few weeks of each year. She not only read the manuscript and offered many valuable suggestions, but also talked with me extensively about her teaching and mentoring experiences. A special thanks to my sister, Kathleen Hoedeman. She has just returned to full-time teaching, has three children, and still found time to answer my plea for input about teaching.

Linda Taylor reviewed the manuscript, inspired me with her vision for teaching, and sent me frequent encouraging e-mails. Patty Taylor is now retired, but was my son's second-grade teacher. She reviewed my list of traits and helped me to clarify and focus my thinking. Although Linda and Patty have many qualities in common, most especially their love of children's literature, they are not related. Roland Smith, a long-ago college friend, experienced superintendent, and now a college professor, shared portions of the manuscript with his classes and offered countless valuable ideas.

The following teachers were more than generous with their valuable time. Their names appear in alphabetical order: Lauren DeAre, Donna Garner, Nettie Griffin, Carol Jago, Jerry Jesness, Adrienne Hamparian Johnson, Sharon Kurolenko, Tessa Lamb, Lucia Leck, Steve Linhardt, Jan Palfenier, Carole Sue Reimann, and Jeanne Wanzek. The following administrators not only reflected on their own teaching experiences in some instances, but also contributed the valuable suggestions on hiring, mentoring, and motivating teachers found in Chapters 7, 8, and 9: Sandra Ahola, Jan Antrim, Pam Conway, Tom Cornell, Cheryl Cozette, Clara Cutts, Gregg Garman, Sharon Huffman, Mike Johnston, Alan Jones, Linda MacKenzie, Kathy Miller, John Patterson, Yvonne Peck, and Sally Roth.

I have worked with many different publishers and editors since my first book was published in 1987. None can compare to Gracia Alkema, the president of Corwin Press, and Robb Clouse, my Acquisitions Editor. They are individuals of uncommon talent and integrity. Gracia's vision for an educational publishing house that would "serve" educators and

the students with whom they work, as well as "sell" books, is a unique one in today's publishing world. She has inspired, mentored, and supported me in ways that no other publisher with whom I have worked has done. I am grateful for her friendship and leadership. Robb Clouse is an author's dream—honest, available, knowledgeable, articulate, and unfailingly kind and good-natured. Gracia and Robb have taken my ideas and made them better, afforded me innumerable opportunities to grow professionally, and been wonderful friends to my husband, Ray, and me. Since my first book with Corwin in 1997, I have been privileged to add 10 titles to their catalog, including *Ten Traits of Highly Effective Teachers*. Who said there wasn't life after school?

About the Author

Elaine K. McEwan is a partner and educational consultant with The McEwan-Adkins Group offering workshops in instructional leadership, team building, raising achievement, reading improvement K–12, and school-community relations. A former teacher, librarian, principal, and assistant superintendent for instruction in a suburban Chicago school district, she is the author of more than 24 books for parents and educators. Her Corwin Press titles include *Leading Your Team to Excellence: How to Make Quality Decisions* (1997), *Seven Steps to Effective Instructional Leadership* (1998), *The Principal's Guide to Attention Deficit Hyperactivity Disorder* (1998), *How to Deal With Parents Who Are Angry, Troubled, Afraid, or Just Plain Crazy* (1998), *The Principal's Guide to Raising Reading Achievement* (1998), *Counseling Tips for Elementary School Principals* (1999) with Jeffrey A. Kottler, *Managing Unmanageable Students: Practical Solutions for Educators* (2000) with Mary Damer, *The Principal's Guide to Raising Math Achievement* (2000), and *Raising Reading Achievement in Middle and High Schools: Five Simple-to-Follow Strategies for Principals* (2001).

Elaine is the education columnist for the *Northwest Explorer* newspaper, a contributing author to several online Web sites for parents, and can be heard on a variety of syndicated radio programs helping parents solve schooling problems. She was honored by the Illinois Principals Association as an outstanding instructional leader, by the Illinois State Board of Education with an Award of Excellence in the Those Who Excel Program, and by the National Association of Elementary School Principals as the National Distinguished Principal from Illinois for 1991. She received her undergraduate degree in education from Wheaton College and advanced degrees in library science (M.A.) and educational administration (Ed.D.) from Northern Illinois University. She lives with her husband and business partner E. Raymond Adkins in Oro Valley, Arizona. Visit Elaine's Web site at www.elainemcewan.com, where you can learn more about her writing and workshops, or contact her directly at emcewan@mindspring.com.

1

Who Is the Effective Teacher?

Those who teach do so because they have known teaching's magical attraction to the spirit, to say nothing of the ego, and have known as students the lengths to which some teachers will go to help others, like themselves, to learn. They know that to convey to others the knowledge of any subject and to do so effectively are two of life's greatest joys.

Banner and Cannon (1997, pp. 133-134)

Jaime Escalante, Marva Collins, Paulo Freire, Maria Montessori, Jesus, and Socrates[1]—what do they have in common? Each is known as a master teacher. Chances are, if we used a contemporary teacher evaluation form to judge their performances, few would get high marks in every category. These master teachers were (or are) more noted for asking diffi-

AUTHOR'S NOTE: I am indebted to the many wonderful educators who shared their opinions, reflections, ideas, and dreams about teaching with me. During the months of January, February, and March of 2001, they kept my inbox filled with e-mail, my post office box filled with snail mail, and my phone messaging system filled with voice mail. Their voices are heard throughout the book. Every individual with whom I communicated is identified by name. To save the busy reader time, I have omitted individual citations for these quotations unless they have appeared in a published work written by the educator, were communicated to me during some other time period than January through March 2001, or appear in a context where the citation is needed for clarity.

cult questions and confronting hypocrisy than for following policy or collaborating with colleagues. Each marched to the beat of a distinctly different drummer. These powerful pedagogues consistently put their students' needs for knowledge, understanding, and empowerment above lofty ambitions, job security, public acclaim, and even personal safety.

They clearly embody the rich complexity of teaching as expressed in Ayers's (1993) definition: "instructing, advising, counseling, organizing, assessing, guiding, goading, showing, managing, modeling, coaching, disciplining, prodding, preaching, persuading, proselytizing, listening, interacting, nursing, and inspiring" (pp. 4-5). Historian Richard Traina (1999) calls teachers like these "memorable." To flesh out in more detail what being a memorable teacher entailed, he examined the autobiographies of 125 prominent Americans from the 19th and 20th centuries. He paid special attention to the descriptions these leaders gave of the teachers whom they admired most. Their descriptions were remarkably consistent: (a) a command of subject matter, (b) a deep caring and concern for students, and (c) a distinctive or memorable attribute or style of teaching. Traina summarizes his findings: "I cannot emphasize enough how powerful this combination of attributes was reported to be. The autobiographers believed their lives were changed by such teachers and professors" (para. 6).

Effective teachers don't always present themselves wrapped in neat and predictable packages, however. They evoke strong and sometimes even negative feelings. Peter Shaker (2001), in an *Education Week* essay titled "Listening to the Music of Teaching," uses the metaphor of music to describe the unique qualities of his high school teachers. Mrs. Anthony, a prototypical old-fashioned Latin teacher, meted out discipline with "a glance or a glare." Shaker remembers her class as having the "mesmerizing quality of . . . a Gregorian chant" (p. 53). Mr. Ford, his calculus teacher, was structured, direct, and unemotional. For Shaker, the memories of his math class brought to mind the discipline of a Bach invention.

Effective teachers don't necessarily need a flamboyant style or entertaining anecdotes to be memorable and influential. Sometimes they just have to be sympathetic and encouraging. Howard Good (2000), journalism professor and author, still remembers his Advanced Placement English teacher with almost reverent awe. Good describes him as "the first adult, besides my parents, to ever show any real interest in me" (para. 5). Good concedes he was an average student, but Mr. Thompson gave him the confidence to become a successful writer.

Effective teachers are often tough and uncompromising. *New York Times* columnist Thomas Friedman (2001) digressed from writing about foreign affairs in his op-ed column and instead eulogized his favorite teacher, Hattie Steinberg. She was Friedman's high school journalism teacher and refused to let him write for the school paper during his junior year, making him sell ads until his writing improved. He describes her as "the toughest teacher I ever had" (para. 5). In spite of her old-fashioned standards, students frequented her classroom most nights after school, Friedman says. "We enjoyed being harangued by her, disciplined by her and taught by her. She was a woman of clarity in an age of uncertainty" (para. 5).

Effective teachers create warm personal bonds that transcend time.

Mitch Albom (1997) described his first sociology class with Morrie Schwartz, a memorable college professor, in his best-selling book, *Tuesdays With Morrie*.

Only a dozen or so students are there, fumbling with notebooks and syllabi. . . . I tell myself it will not be easy to cut a class this small. Maybe I shouldn't take it.

"Mitchell?" Morrie says, reading from the attendance list.

I raise a hand.

"Do you prefer Mitch? Or is Mitchell better?"

I have never been asked this by a teacher. I do a double take at this guy in his yellow turtleneck and green corduroy pants, the silver hair that falls on his forehead. He is smiling.

"Mitch," I say. "Mitch is what my friends call me."

"Well, Mitch it is then," Morrie says, as if closing a deal.

"And, Mitch?"

"Yes?"

"I hope one day you will think of me as your friend." (pp. 24-25)

The memory of this first class with Morrie haunted Albom's memory for 20 years. He finally sought out Morrie, only to find that he was terminally ill. In the waning months of Morrie's life, Albom goes back to class every Tuesday with his dying professor. This time the subject is life—not sociology.

Who Is the Effective Teacher?

When one considers these unique and compelling instructors, the very idea of defining an effective teacher may seem altogether presumptuous. The pedagogues we have enumerated elevated teaching to an art. They were masters—remembered through time for their effect not only on students, but frequently on society as well.

Nevertheless, scholars have tried for over a century to create a schema that would describe and codify effective teachers. One early researcher asked a group of students to identify the characteristics that distinguished the teachers from whom they learned the most from those whom they liked the most. Four characteristics of teachers who were successful at getting the respondents to learn a lot were named by at least 10% of the students questioned:

1. Making greater demands of the students

2. More teaching skill

3. More knowledge of subject matter

4. Better discipline (Kratz, 1896, pp. 413-418)

Although these students spoke from firsthand knowledge regarding the ability of their teachers to get results, their opinions were largely discounted. At the turn of the 20th century, the perfect teacher was thought to be "a good person—a role model who met the community ideal" (Borich, 2000, p. 1). In the minds of most, whether or not students learned depended on the efforts of the students themselves—not the talents of their teachers.

More than 30 years later, however, Barr and Emans (1930) reintroduced a model of teacher effectiveness based on the achievement of students. Again the psychological-characteristics profile of an effective teacher prevailed, and their theory lay dormant for decades. Those who studied teachers looked instead for "artists" among the population of prospective and current teachers or focused solely on their backgrounds and experiences. One of the earliest large-scale studies of teachers' characteristics (Ryans, 1960) found that "superior intellectual abilities, above-average school achievement, good emotional adjustment, generosity in the appraisal of the behavior and motives of other persons, early experiences in caring for children, and a history of teaching in the family" were some of the characteristics that applied "very generally to teachers judged by various kinds and sets of criteria to be outstanding" (p. 366). The search for "the effective teacher" continued to focus on what teachers were like, rarely on what they did or should do during the act of teaching. Little wonder that in the early 1960s, the newly published *Handbook of Research on Teaching* concluded that there was no substantive field of research on teaching (Gage, 1963).

The Coleman Report further reinforced the notion that teaching quality mattered in terms of students' success in school (Coleman, 1966). In response to Coleman's bleak assessment, researchers in the early 1970s began to study teaching behavior in more intense and experimental ways.

Investigators began to look at far more than characteristics like years of experience or amount of education. They asked students, experienced teachers, principals, and college professors to list the behaviors associated with good teaching. They entered classrooms and did intensive case studies about what they observed over extended periods of time. They rated large numbers of teachers on specific traits and then examined whether any of the traits were associated with teachers whose students were more motivated or had higher academic achievement. They identified teachers whose students consistently achieved higher than students in other classrooms and closely compared what these teachers might have done differently from the teachers of low-achieving students. Finally, they trained teachers to use various strategies to teach the same lesson and determined which approach was most effective in promoting learning.

The definition of an effective teacher began to change as the emphasis shifted from what teachers were to what they did, and what effects those behaviors had on student achievement. Researchers like Berliner (1985), Brophy and Good (1974), Hunter (1984), Rosenshine (1971), and Soar and Soar (1979) developed checklists and models that defined specific behaviors associated with students' achievement. Practitioners, delighted with these seemingly definitive answers, eagerly developed workshops to train teachers in a variety of seven-step lesson models (Hunter, 1979; Manatt, 1985; Rosenshine, 1983). These models, while undeniably effective for many kinds of students and a wide variety of learning tasks, did not encompass the totality of teaching every subject to every student in the K–12 continuum. Some observers argued that "teaching is a dynamic, evolving activity that cannot be neatly packaged or succinctly defined . . . [often] characterized by mess and noise, by people—lots of people—by caring and heartache, and most of all, by uncertainty and vagueness" (Goodwin, 1987, p. 30). Others asserted that "there is no such thing as a behavioral definition of teaching and there never can be. We can never simply watch a person in action and be sure that something called teaching is going on" (Jackson, 1968, p. 77).

Science or Art?

The tension that exists between teaching as a science (i.e., a skill or technique that can be taught with training) and teaching as an art (i.e., a natural aptitude that cannot be taught), between answers and ambiguity, confronts principals and teachers daily. There are other troubling dilemmas as well. Which counts more—what students learn about content or that lessons of caring are taught? Which is better—direct instruction or discovery learning? When Gage (1985) was asked if teaching was an art or a science, he replied, "The answer is yes" (p. 53). To the question of what counts more—content or caring—my answer is also yes. An ample body of research exists showing that content and caring are not mutually exclusive commodities; effective teachers emphasize both, and both content and caring contribute to the outcomes and accountability we desire. To the question of whether the most effective instruction is structured or nonstructured, my answer is both. The students, the subject, and the desired learning outcome are the best determinants of what kind of instruction to use, and the results of that instruction in terms of student learning should determine its effectiveness.

A Matter of Definition

In light of the aforementioned ambiguities, defining an effective teacher in a mere 10 traits is a challenging task—but not an impossible one. To make the task more manageable, I have taken some literary license with the meaning of *trait*. Webster's defines it as "a distinguishing quality or characteristic" (McKechnie, 1983, p. 1936). The traits that I describe in the chapters ahead are not as singular, simple, or straightforward as implied by the dictionary definition. The traits I chose, although easily summarized in a word or phrase, are definitely more akin to concepts or constellations than single traits. But, *The Ten Concepts (or Constellations) of Highly Effective Teachers* doesn't quite have the same ring to it as *The Ten Traits of Highly Effective Teachers*. I hope that you will be able to momentarily suspend Webster's definition of *trait* and live with my more comprehensive interpretation, that is, at least until you finish reading the book.

Moreover, for purposes of our discussion in the chapters ahead, *effective* will not be used exclusively. Rather, *good, successful, master, outstanding, superior, excellent,* and *skillful* will be used interchangeably—not only to make for less repetitive and more interesting reading, but also to accommodate the variety of ways educators describe teachers whom they consider to be the very best. The understood definition of *effective* along with the aforementioned terms will be Webster's: "producing a decided, decisive, or desired effect (result or outcome), producing an intended effort" (McKechnie, 1983, p. 577). The time, effort, and money that we expend on "teaching" must produce an intended effort.

In contrast, the understood definition of the verb *teach* will be expanded beyond the dictionary definition. Webster lists the following as synonyms for teach: "impart, direct, instruct, inform, counsel, advocate, educate, inculcate, enlighten, advise, and indoctrinate" (McKechnie, 1983, pp. 1870-1871). Although the nature of the content or the skill and knowledge levels of students often dictate that teachers must be directive and assertive in their teaching methodologies, Webster did not take into account that the acts of imparting, informing, and directing do not always produce the results and outcomes we desire. As those who have been teachers will attest, the learner must be an active participant in the process. Thus to teach also means to motivate, to facilitate, to encourage, to nurture, to lead, to cajole, and to collaborate as well as to instruct and to inform. As Hamachek (1999) observed "Effective teachers are, in a sense, 'total' teachers. They seem able to adjust to the shifting tides of classroom life and students' needs, and to do what has to be done to reach, and thereby teach, different students in a variety of circumstances" (p. 206).

The Great Debate

Joyce and Weil (1996) frame the competing demands of teaching as an ongoing debate between an emphasis on basic school subjects and a concentration on the nurturance of thinking. They suggest that we usually instruct and direct when we teach to minimum competencies—a necessary role of every teacher at some point in that teacher's work with a given group of students—but surely not representative of the totality of teaching. The master teacher, they assert, ought also to be concerned with creativity, problem-solving and critical-thinking skills. They wisely observe and warn, however, that

> the argument is usually carried on as if to do one would sacrifice the other. Otherwise reasonable people argue that if we teach the sciences inductively, we will lose coverage of the subjects, or that we will undermine values if we encourage students to think about them, or even that drill and practice will always and surely dull the mind. These arguments reductio ad absurdum, riding on deeply felt emotions and expressed in hyperbole, are hangers-on from the poverty of our past, when it seemed almost too much to afford the barest education. The skills of reading, the study of values, the analytic tools of scholars, and the nurture of intuition are compatible, and we can and should teach them all simultaneously. (p. 142)

Make no mistake, however. An effective teacher in the flesh is not a paragon of pedagogical perfection who can be all things to all students. All of the 10 traits occur on a continuum; no teacher is uniformly strong in every trait. New teachers need time to mature. Experienced teachers need to be energized and empowered. Furthermore, teachers are human. They have personal tragedies and illnesses that can sap their energies, destroy their desire, and sometimes impair their effectiveness. So, the following 10 traits are offered, not merely as criteria against which teachers might measure themselves or be evaluated by supervisors, but also as a set of goals to which all teachers can aspire. In the end, however, anyone who has ever been a teacher knows that these 10 traits are in reality the ongoing lessons or disciplines of teaching. As Gilbert Highet (1976) wisely observed,

> When I started teaching, I thought it would become easier as I went along. Now I know it does not. In one way, teaching as a profession is scarcely comparable to medicine or the church. After twenty years' experience, a doctor knows an enlarged spleen when he feels one, and a priest or minister knows what to

say to a mourner or a sinner; but the average teacher has no such thorough grasp of his craft, because it is constantly changing and he himself must change with it. (p. 75)

The Ten Traits of Highly Effective Teachers

Banner and Cannon (1997), in their introduction to *The Elements of Teaching,* describe the difficulty all educators face when attempting to define great teaching: "We think we know great teaching when we encounter it, yet we find it impossible to say precisely what has gone into making it great" (p. 3). The coauthors, both outstanding teachers in their own right, do not, however, let this obstacle deter them from identifying nine specific qualities of character and mind desirable in all teachers. I am no less reticent than Banner and Cannon when I suggest the following 10 traits of highly effective teachers.

Personal Traits That Signify Character: What the Effective Teacher Is

Trait 1. Mission-Driven and Passionate

The effective teacher is mission-driven, feeling a "call" to teach as well as a passion to help students learn and grow.

> *To be a passionate teacher is to be someone in love with a field of knowledge, deeply stirred by issues and ideas that challenge our world, drawn to the dilemmas and potentials of the young people who come into class each day—or captivated by all of these.*
>
> Fried (1995, p. 1)

Lucia Leck is a first-grade teacher in a suburban midwestern town. She is the mother of three grown children, an avid naturalist, and has the patience of a saint. Perhaps that is because her first calling came from God. She confesses that she wasn't called to teaching—at least not in the beginning. She entered the religious community of Benedictines at St. Scholastica Monastery in Duluth immediately after high school, and there she was told she would be trained as a teacher. "I had no other choice," she says.

She freely admits that she was not at all passionate about teaching in the beginning. "I just hoped to survive—survive from 8:00 a.m. until noon, and then from noon to the end of the day." She was following orders and wasn't thrilled about them.

"I came into 'passionate' through the back door," she laughingly shares. "Somewhere in my life journey, the desire to make a difference grew. I discovered I cared deeply about making an impact on children's lives." That desire propelled Lucia to reenter teaching, after staying at home to raise her children. She has no lack of passion today. "Teaching children to read has become everything for me. I see it as the tool they need to be lifelong learners," she explains. Lucia will be retiring in a couple of years. She will leave teaching knowing she has given all she can to the profession. She was a slow starter, but she is a strong finisher.

Trait 2: Positive and Real

The highly effective teacher is positive and real, demonstrating the qualities of caring, empathy, respect, and fairness in relationships with students, parents, and colleagues.

Good teaching cannot be reduced to technique; good teaching comes from the identity and integrity of the teacher.

Palmer (1998, p. 10)

Linda Taylor teaches high school special education students in a rural northern Michigan community. Students arrive on her doorstep needing extra doses of caring, empathy, respect, and fairness, in addition to ample amounts of supportive and systematic instruction. Most have attended multiple schools since their initial placement in special education, and they know firsthand how it feels to be unloved, misunderstood, or ignored. One day Linda asked their opinions regarding the importance of these qualities. Oh, she didn't phrase the question quite like that, but instead asked her students to describe their schooling experiences before they enrolled in her class as freshmen. Here are some selected observations from just a few of her students.[2]

Jennifer: School doesn't give kids a chance.

Sam: The more you are told "you are bad" the more you believe it. School is more worried about punishment and making more rules, instead of how to really help kids.

Susan: Kids don't understand and the teachers don't explain better.

Jennifer: Teachers should sit with kids and find out what they are really like inside. The school doesn't know who I really am inside.

Ron: Teachers don't pay attention to the kids to learn about the kids. Teachers need to get to know students better, and it should be done earlier. Teachers expect kids to do work they are not capable of doing, but the teachers don't know the kids individually and well enough to even know that.

Sam: Teachers think that you can do the work but are just refusing to do it. That you are lazy. That you don't care.

Aileen: Everyone else gets done first and I feel awful always being the last one done.

Sam: I am so slow but when I am at CTC [Career Training Center] I skip lots, guess, anything, just so I can hand my paper in with the others and not hold everyone else up. CTC doesn't care that I am good with working on the cars. They grade on the paperwork. They never grade me on what I do best.

Linda not only teaches her students to read, write, and do math; she also gives them daily lessons in caring, empathy, respect, and fairness.

Trait 3: A Teacher-Leader

The highly effective teacher is a "teacher-leader" who positively affects the lives of students, parents, and colleagues.

Leadership—any kind of leadership—is concerned with helping.
                                        Pellicer & Anderson (1995, p. 22)

Marsha Arest is a high school Spanish teacher in an upscale suburban New York community. She makes an impression wherever she focuses her high-energy efforts. Whether she's coaching a new teacher in how to communicate more effectively with parents, organizing staff-development opportunities for her colleagues, or developing leadership skills among students, she is constantly making a difference. The list of extracurricular activities to which Marsha has brought her leadership talents for over 30 years would stagger most educators.

Marsha loves change, however; it motivates and energizes her. She is always looking for ways to improve her classroom, her school, her students, or herself. She does confess that at times she is considered "difficult" by her colleagues because she pushes too hard. "So, I have had to become more aware of others' learning curves. Just like a good teacher would." Marsha definitely qualifies as a "good" teacher.

Teaching Traits That Get Results: What the Effective Teacher Does

Trait 4: With-It-Ness

The highly effective teacher demonstrates with-it-ness—the state of being on top of, tuned in to, aware of, and in complete control of three critical facets of classroom life:

1. The management and organization of the classroom

2. The engagement of students

3. The management of time

> With-it-ness doesn't seem a noble enough word for such an immense task. This is the juggling trait—how to keep all of the balls in the air at the same time. (Lucia Leck)

I loved to visit Mark Stevenson's[3] upper-grade classroom. It functioned like a well-oiled machine. Students knew exactly what they were supposed to do when they came into his classroom every day: how to pass in papers and tests, where to get supplies when they ran out, what to do if they needed help and the teacher was busy, how to respond to signals from the teacher to get their attention, how to purchase lunch tickets, where to put homework that was due, the procedure for returning library books, how to copy assignments into their daily planner, and how to organize into teams for team competitions or cooperative groups. They even got the plants watered, the floor picked up, and the board erased every day. They knew exactly how to set up their papers for math and how to prepare the final draft of a writing assignment. They had steps for proofreading each other's assignments, checking their daily math quizzes, and studying in small groups for tests using the teacher-prepared study guides. When the dismissal bell rang, they had their books stacked on their desks and their assignment notebooks filled out. There are those seemingly creative and carefree souls who rail against such regimentation and routine. "Boring," they whine. "Too confining." Those are the ineffective teachers who seldom have the time or energy to finish what they've planned for a day. They are so exhausted from dealing with the repetitive questions and relentless problems that continually occur when students haven't mastered classroom routines, expectations, and procedures, they have no time for stirring discussions and inspiring lessons.

Mr. Stevenson left nothing to chance. He used the same steps to teach classroom procedures that are described in the book, *How to Be an Effective Teacher* (Wong & Wong, 1998, pp. 174-176). In fact, Mr. Stevenson could have written the book. He took time (as much as was needed) at the beginning of every school year to explain, rehearse, and reinforce all of the procedures he wanted students to use. He didn't assume that just because his students were almost ready to head off to middle school they would automatically know how to do these things. In fact, he didn't care how they had done things in the past. In his class, he wanted them done in his way and done automatically and efficiently. After teaching the procedures, he even tested students to make sure that they had mastered them. Once his procedures were explained, rehearsed, reinforced, and mastered, he didn't want to worry about them ever again. He had, in the words of Jane Stallings (1985), "gotten the show on the road" (p. 3).

Only then did Mr. Stevenson begin to teach content. Once he started, he never stopped. Students who had been off-task in other classrooms were suddenly models of decorum. Laggards who never finished homework in other grades soon made the honor roll. He didn't have to nag to the extent that many of his colleagues did; his students always knew exactly what to do. Interestingly enough, many of them came back regularly from middle and high school to visit. They loved to report their academic successes. They knew why they were doing so well; it was the superb organizational habits and work ethic they had learned from Mr. Stevenson. Not to mention the math, writing, reading, and thinking skills they had also mastered.

Trait 5: Style

The effective teacher exhibits a personal unique style, bringing drama, enthusiasm, liveliness, humor, charisma, creativity, and novelty to teaching.

Be willing to be yourself, not another teacher who might be popular, or one who teaches in a way you wish you could.

Sharon Kurolenko

Every educator has heard of Jaime Escalante—the "Stand and Deliver" math teacher. If you haven't read the book (Mathews, 1988), you've seen the movie with Edward James Olmos in the title role. The story of Escalante's success in getting barrio youth to master AP Calculus is legendary. In 1987, Garfield High School, in a predominantly Latino lower- and middle-income area in Los Angeles, registered 129 students to take the AP Calculus exam. Sixty-six percent of those students received a score of 3 or better (Mathews, 1988). This achievement placed Garfield among the top U.S. public high school AP Calculus programs.

Escalante is the quintessential teacher with style. I have chosen to feature him as an exemplar of this trait for a number of reasons:

1. He clearly has substance (i.e., knowledge of content and instructional effectiveness) to go along with his style.

2. His style is not an artifice, but a genuine expression of who he is as a person and a teacher.

3. His visibility as a national figure increases the likelihood that you have a more complete context in which to think about style as it relates to highly effective teachers.

4. His style completely encompasses all of the aspects named in the previous description.

5. Escalante's story demonstrates the downside of an overabundance of "style"—petty jealousies and turf wars with administrators and fellow teachers.

Jay Mathews, Los Angeles bureau chief of the *Washington Post*, tells Escalante's story in his book *Escalante: The Best Teacher in America*.

His thick brown fingers swept the air when he lectured and ground chalk into the blackboard with an audible crack. He had a stocky build, a large square head with prominent jaw, and a widening bald spot covered with a few stray hairs, like a threadbare victory wreath on a Bolivian Caesar. He looked oddly like the school mascot, a gruff bulldog, and exuded a sense of mischief that made me, and I discovered later, many others want to keep a close eye on him. (Mathews, 1988, p. 3)

Escalante's style includes his penchant for mixing up his English with bits of Spanish and two Bolivian Indian dialects as well as his constant use of "invented" words and phrases—"Escalantese," if you will. Only his students understand the "shorthand" language. For example, "Mickey Mouse" refers to classes like "woodworking, plastics, marching band, cheerleading, or any sport that takes time from math." "Take your break and don't come back" is Escalante's way of saying, "get out of class." When a student repeatedly fails tests, he/she must see Escalante after school every day to get back on track; he/she is said to be in "intensive care" (Mathews, 1988, pp. 307-308).

Escalante also uses a repertoire of oft-repeated phrases that constantly communicate his expectations to students in humorous and often self-deprecating ways.

- ■ "The only thing you got to do over here [speaking to students who had transferred to Garfield from another school in Los Angeles] you got to work with *ganas* [the Spanish word for "urge" as in the urge to succeed, to achieve, to grow]. You don't have to have a high IQ, not like the ones that have one twenty, one forty IQ. Myself, I have a negative IQ. So the only thing I require of you is *ganas*" (as quoted in Mathews, 1988, p. 249).

- ■ "Determination plus hard work plus concentration equals success, which equals *ganas*" (p. 191).

- ■ "Calculus need not be made easy; it is easy already" (p. 115).

Escalante's style has a way of getting into students' heads and motivating them to break out of their prisons of academic failure. His style also has a way of goading fellow educators to think about issues they would rather not confront.

Trait 6: Motivational Expertise

The highly effective teacher is a motivator par excellence who believes in his or her own ability to make a difference in the lives of students and relentlessly presses and pursues students to maintain the highest possible behavioral and academic expectations.

I see a teacher as a motivator above all else.

Patty Taylor

Jeanne Wanzek's school sits in the middle of a cornfield. This pastoral setting camouflages the high-energy pace in her classroom. She relentlessly presses and pursues her second-grade students. Under her tutelage, every student's potential is realized. Her passion for perfecting her instructional expertise will take Jeanne back to graduate school next year to pursue a doctorate in special education while she works at the Center for Reading at the University of Texas in Houston.

> I have learned in my teaching that with the right kind of instruction students will rise to any expectations a teacher sets. I have seen students demonstrate very different behavior and academic work depending on who the teacher is and how the expectations are communicated. It is important, however, that the expectations be coupled with excellent instruction. Excellent instruction without high expectations will not push students to their full potential. Of course, high expectations without the appropriate instruction to give students the skills and knowledge they need will only cause them frustration.

As a former special education teacher, Jeanne is distressed by the recent trend to lower expectation for students with disabilities.

> Students can learn, particularly the lowest students, anything if you teach, actually teach, them how to do it. Their success is all the motivation they need. Many times we don't change our teaching approach when a student isn't learning; we lower the expectations for that student. We shorten the spelling list, require fewer pages of work, or teach a watered down lesson. The student is then "successful," but what has really happened is that we have reduced our expectations to make a poor curricu-

lum or poor teaching methods look better. Instead, we should change our teaching to make the high expectations possible. Many times the learning will be almost effortless for students if the teaching is well-designed; students love that kind of success.

Trait 7: Instructional Effectiveness

The highly effective teacher is an instructional virtuoso: a skilled communicator with a repertoire of essential abilities, behaviors, models, and principles that lead all students to learning.

Choosing the most important instructional skill is like choosing which component is the most important in the operation of an automobile. Clearly a car needs an engine, a transmission, and brakes, and cannot be operated without all of them.

Jerry Jesness

One has to be an instructional virtuoso to successfully teach five groups of hormonally charged eighth graders every day. Adrienne Hamparian Johnson's 120 students are heterogeneously grouped, with each class containing a mix of gifted and talented, above average, average, below average, mildly learning disabled, severely learning disabled, emotionally or behaviorally challenged, and bilingual students. Her school, located in the far western suburbs of Chicago, has a highly diverse student body. Nearly one half (45%) of the students come from families where English is a second language. More than one third of them are on free or reduced-price lunches.

Adrienne is an instructional virtuoso. A finalist for Teacher of the Year in Illinois (1998), she is a whirling dervish of ideas, methods, and strategies. She exudes energy. "I have discovered that all of my students can do well at something, and it's part of my mission to encourage them to find those strengths," says Adrienne. Her specialty is differentiated instruction and she is a master at asking just the right questions. Like the porridge that Goldilocks selected at the cottage of the three bears, Adrienne's questions are always "just right." Not too easy—students need high expectations. Not too hard—students need to succeed. But just right. No matter what their level, each student is required to stretch a little to jump over the bar. Adrienne constantly conveys a sense of expectations and confidence in her students' abilities. She offers an extensive menu of alternative activities and assignments (developed jointly with students) that are intended to meet the needs of her gifted and talented students, but she places no restrictions on who can substitute one of the higher-level assignments for a regular one. She reports that her average and below-average students frequently choose from the "hard menu" as well, reaching well beyond their comfort levels and usually making the grade.

During a recent school year, nearly one half of Adrienne's students had poems published (her school was listed in the top 10% of all the schools who entered the contest); one pupil won first place in the Congressional District for a letter dealing with national social issues; and a third pupil won first prize in a countywide writing contest asking for solutions to the problem of violence. Her students have won numerous awards with their interdisciplinary projects—a technology award for the Web site they developed for the community's historical museum and recognition from the Adler Planetarium and National Aeronautics and Space Administration (NASA) for their Mars Millennium project. When students enter Adrienne's classroom, they immediately sense her unconditional positive regard for their level of mastery and their potential for success. They respond to her instructional expertise with achievement—not only in her classroom, but also in their community.

Intellectual Traits That Demonstrate Knowledge, Curiosity, and Awareness: What and How an Effective Teacher Thinks

Trait 8: Book Learning

The highly effective teacher has a sound knowledge of content (the structure of the discipline) and outcomes (what the school, district, or state has determined is essential for students to know).

I teach in order to make a difference, to make children feel the power of knowledge.

Marsha Arest

Carol Jago has taught English at the middle and high school levels for 26 years. She also directs the California Reading and Literature Project at UCLA and writes a weekly education column for the *Los Angeles Times*. Carol is the personification of Banner and Cannon's (1997) teacher who is "able to relate knowledge to life, to all human experience" (p. 12). She reveres the classics and is determined that the current generation of students will not be deprived of what they have to offer.

In her book, *With Rigor for All: Teaching the Classics to Contemporary Students,* she concedes that inspiring the average teenager to read *The Odyssey* and *Julius Caesar* is a challenging assignment.

> Apart from a rare few, the young people I teach do not pick up classic literature with much enthusiasm. At first they groan, "Three hundred pages of poetry!" Then they moan, "I can't do it. Not one word of what I read last night makes sense." They always hope that if they complain enough, I will abandon the text for something simpler. Instead I assure them that over the next few weeks I am going to show them how to unlock this book for themselves. I let students know that the satisfaction they will feel at meeting this textual challenge is an intellectual reward that I would not for the world deny them. (Jago, 2000, p. 4)

Carol genuinely loves reading and literature (personal communication, February 12, 2001) and finds that even though she assigns the same books year after year, the students "make it different every time around" (Jago, 2000, p. 3). She speculates that

> without determined high school English teachers, love and respect for literature would die out. Not many students stumble upon the works of Thomas Hardy on their parents' bookshelves or choose to peek between the covers if they do. But for as long as teachers continue to make enduring stories come to life for young readers, the study of literature will remain a vital pursuit. (p. 5)

Trait 9: Street Smarts

The highly effective teacher has knowledge of the students, the school, and the community in which that teacher is teaching and uses this knowledge to solve problems in the instructional setting.

> *As soon as I find myself not treasuring those relationships, I will know that is my sign to find a new career.*
>
> Steve Linhardt

Although he is inches taller today than when he was in middle school, Steve Linhardt is the same genuine young man I knew when he and my son started a lawn-mowing business in our neighborhood. An honors graduate of Indiana University and about to receive his M.A. in Educational Leadership, Steve has been teaching for seven years at his high school alma mater in the suburbs of Chicago. Steve knows the school and community intimately, but gaining knowledge about his students is an ongoing adventure for him.

> Getting to know one's students well is an incredible challenge at the high school level. I have 140 students each day, and I only get to see them for 50 minutes. I am jealous of my wife because she has 21 third graders and gets to be with them all day. Obviously in a third grade classroom you can get to know students much more fully and then understand where they are coming from. Personally, the students are my favorite part of teaching, though. I love history and politics, but I enjoy being with the kids even more. Relationships with students are why I chose to be a teacher, and they will be the reason that I will stay in the profession.

Trait 10: A Mental Life

The highly effective teacher has a substantive thought life that includes the abilities to be the following:

1. *Metacognitive:* able to read one's own mental state and then assess how that state will affect one's present and future performance

2. *Strategic:* able to think aloud and model strategic learning for students

3. *Reflective:* able to think about personal teaching behaviors for the purposes of self-growth

4. *Communicative:* able to articulate ideas, issues, beliefs, and values about the act of teaching with colleagues, students, and parents

5. *Responsive:* able to "flex" to the changing needs and demands of the profession

Knowing who you are and what you are about is like the ground you stand on while you're teaching.

Lucia Leck

Kathleen Hoedeman eloquently summarizes the texture and complexity of this final trait of highly effective teachers. The suburban Pittsburgh school district in which she is employed places a high value on customer satisfaction and quality interactions with parents. Kathleen's ability to reflect on her teaching and to communicate meaningfully with parents, as well as colleagues, is an essential aspect of total effectiveness.

We teach who we are. Teaching, like any truly human activity, emerges from one's inwardness, for better or worse. Thus, knowing myself is as crucial to good teaching as knowing my students and my subject. If I am confident in my mastery of the subject, confident in my ability to communicate, confident in the value of the learning I am promoting, I will not fail. The respect I have for myself gives me the freedom to respect my students. The high expectations I place on my own performance gives me permission to expect much from those I teach. Confidence in my own abilities as an educator lets me invite questions and criticism from parents, students, and other professionals and grow from their input.

Recapping Chapter 1

Chapter 1 has asked and I hope begun to answer the question: Who is the highly effective teacher? You have been introduced to 10 individual traits grouped into three categories:

1. Personal traits that signify character

2. Teaching traits that get results

3. Intellectual traits that demonstrate knowledge, curiosity, and awareness

Figure 1.1 displays the 10 traits in a reproducible graphic organizer. As mentioned in the Preface, you will find numerous graphic organizers throughout the book; a complete set of all them can be found in

Figure 1.1. The Ten Traits of Highly Effective Teachers

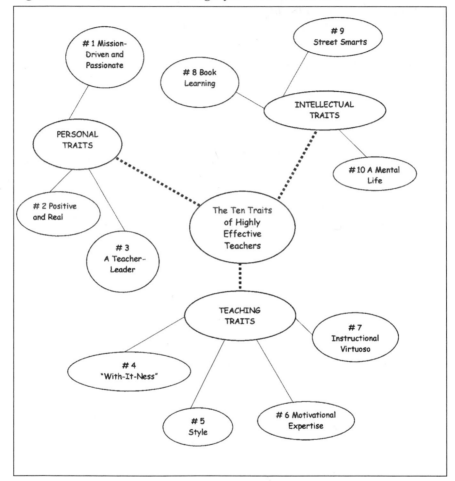

Resource A. Resource B contains a complete list of the 10 traits along with their definitions.

Teachers who are living, breathing exemplars of the 10 traits in their classrooms, schools, and communities are notable and often unique individuals. Many have been honored with awards or recognition. However, for each highly effective teacher who is publicly recognized, there are hundreds of thousands who are known only to their students. These are the teachers like Patty Taylor, my son Patrick's second-grade teacher, now retired. Patrick once wrote an essay about her, describing the part she played in helping him to become an honors student. Patrick read 1,087 books while he was in her class. That was a remarkable achievement for him, but what was even more remarkable, is that Mrs. Taylor motivated him to keep on reading, appreciated the simple reports he wrote about the books he read, listened to his oral accounts of them, and recorded each and every one on a chart for all to see. Teachers like Mrs. Taylor are unsung heroines (or heroes), remembered not for their dramatic or spectacular achievements, but for the little things they do so faithfully day after day—the quiet conversations, the simple words of encouragement, and the skillfully executed lessons that have brought academic success, personal self-worth, and a love of learning to their students.

What's Ahead?

In the chapters ahead you will find detailed descriptions of each of the 10 traits. There are examples, anecdotes, first-person reflections of teachers—both new and experienced—and research findings (where applicable) that link the traits to student achievement. As you read, take some time to "talk back" to me, the author. You may even want to tweak my list a bit and develop your own customized set of 10 traits—one that is more meaningful to you. I encourage you to do that. I have provided a do-it-yourself graphic organizer, Form 1.1, for just that purpose. I can assure you that the experience of thinking about the traits, particularly as they relate to the many teachers you have known, will give you a renewed and deeper appreciation for the contributions of highly effective teachers.

Notes

1. The following books provide further information about each of the teachers cited: Escalante (Mathews, 1988); Collins (Collins & Tamarkin, 1982); Freire (1998); Montessori (1912); Jesus (Lockyer, 1991); and Socrates (Seeskin, 1986).

2. The names of Linda's students have been changed to protect their privacy. They are students with the following disabilities: hearing

Form 1.1. A Do-It-Yourself Ten Traits of Highly Effective Teachers

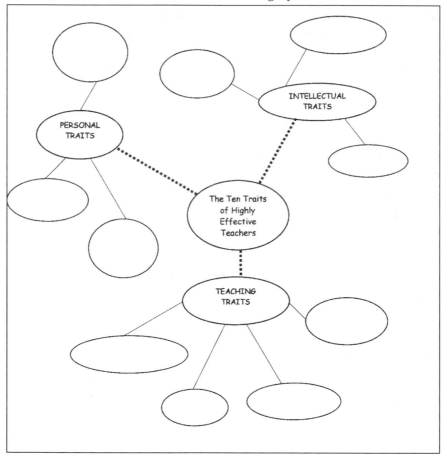

impaired, learning disabled, behavior disordered, and educably mentally impaired.

3. Mark Stevenson is a composite of many highly effective teachers whom I have known and with whom I have worked in my nearly 30 years in education. Having served in four different job roles in several different school districts, I have seen the best. Mark is not intended to describe any single teacher I have known.

2

Personal Traits That Indicate Character

What an Effective Teacher Is

A conversation between Sir Thomas More and Richard Rich, a younger associate, regarding Richard's future plans:

More: *Why not be a teacher? You'd be a fine teacher. Perhaps even a great one.*

Rich: *And if I was, who would know it?*

More: *You, your pupils, your friends, God. Not a bad public, that. . . . Oh, and a quiet life.*

Bolt (A Man for All Seasons, 1962, p. 6)

Why does anyone, whether college age or middle age, decide to become a teacher? Teaching is often a lonely and isolated profession (Sarason, 1971), fraught with uncertainties and a "shadowed social standing" (Lortie, 1975, p. 10), confused about its purpose (Lieberman & Miller, 1984), and characterized by mess and noise (Goodwin, 1987). Many college students are actively discouraged from choosing a teaching career by their parents, peers, and professors (Olson, 1997). Yet, every year, thousands of young people do choose to pursue a teaching credential. Many more opt to join a volunteer teaching program that bypasses preservice training and student teaching, replacing the traditional route to the classroom with a summer training program and follow-up college courses. Thousands of others leave careers as engineers, investment bankers, and delivery truck drivers for the privilege of being called "teacher."

There are many reasons that an individual may choose to teach: attractive hours and long summer vacations; a family tradition of teaching; the effect of a favorite professor; or in many cases, the desire to make a difference. As an elementary school principal, I yearly interviewed 24 or more applicants for teaching positions. I always asked them why they wanted to be a teacher, and specifically why they wanted to teach at Lincoln School. I heard many inspiring and heartwarming stories over the years, but one reply was unforgettable. The candidate had substituted for us frequently and I hoped that her reasons for wanting to join our staff might include the friendly and supportive climate in our school. I speculated that perhaps she would like to be part of the successful school-improvement initiatives that were bringing us notice in the community. I was prepared for just about any response but the one she gave: "I need the benefits." I was ready to call off the interview on the spot, but I gave her the courtesy of completing it. I didn't hire this individual, because I was looking for passion and she was concerned only with practicality. I wanted to see evidence of what Gill calls the first commandment of good teaching: "Thou shalt not become a teacher unless you feel a calling to this mother of all professions" (Gill, 1998, p. 5). This applicant did have a mission, but it had nothing to do with success for our students.

Trait 1: Mission-Driven and Passionate

The highly effective teacher is mission-driven, feeling a call to teach as well as a passion to help students learn and grow.

> *Actually, I left marketing research because I felt like I wasn't doing anything to contribute to society except trying to force people to buy stuff they didn't need! The experience makes me appreciate teaching all the more!*
>
> Nettie Griffin

When *calling* is used to describe a career choice, one immediately thinks of a religious vocation. You may wonder whether this first trait of highly effective teachers should include the concept of *calling* or possibly doubt that people actually feel a calling to teach. The term is often used in the educational literature, however, and many of the teachers whom I interviewed in preparation for this book used the term to describe their own feelings of passion for the profession. Serow (1994) writes that

> those who say they are called to teach display significantly greater enthusiasm and commitment to the idea of a teaching career, are more mindful of its potential impact on other people, are less concerned about the sacrifices that such a career might entail, and are more willing to accept the extra duties that often accompany the teacher's role. (p. 65)

Teaching is undeniably difficult and discouraging work at times— especially if one is teaching in schools where resources are limited and large numbers of students are at-risk of failure.

Teachers With a Calling

I love Spanish. It speaks from my heart and soul. So to be able to work with kids and speak a language I love—what more could one ask?
                                                                Marsha Arest

Lauren DeAre feels a calling. If she didn't, she would have quit after her first week on the job. Her school doesn't quite qualify as "oppressive and mean" (Kohl, 1984, p. 7), but certainly is not the most welcoming environment for a brand-new teacher with a passion to make a difference. She is 23 and a recent graduate of the University of Wisconsin with a double major in English literature and Spanish language. Although she was hired to be part of a bilingual program in the urban Southwestern district where she teaches second grade, no one has taken the time to explain the program's organization and goals to her. The principal is a weak instructional leader who is unfamiliar with lower-primary curriculum and teachers. His public appearances are rare. She was given the key to her classroom and told that "whatever is in there is what you're supposed to teach."

Only her calling keeps her going. It was after living in Ecuador for a short time that Lauren suddenly realized she was in the wrong country. If she wanted to make a difference, she reasoned, she really ought to begin in her own backyard. She returned to the United States and immediately signed up with Teach for America. She has faced more frustration in her first semester than I faced in my entire teaching career, but she knows what is most important: her students and their learning. In spite of the roadblocks, Lauren is determined to become a successful teacher. "I couldn't quit," she says. "There are days I haven't felt like going to school, but I could *never* leave my students like that. I hear their stories of what the substitutes make them do and how they are treated."

In addition to a calling, highly effective teachers have a passion to be with students and to help them be successful. Jeanne Wanzek, for several years a special education teacher, and now in a second-grade classroom, finds that over the years her mission has been refined and refocused. Effective teachers continue to grow into their roles and enlarge the scope of their missions as they sense the enormity of the challenge and gain further knowledge and skills. They become "deeply stirred by issues and ideas that challenge our world, drawn to the dilemmas and potentials of the young people who come into class every day—or captivated by all of these" (Fried, 1995, p. 1). Jeanne Wanzek puts it this way:

> Although I went into teaching with a mission to affect children's lives, I didn't really know what I wanted to do until I saw some of the problems in education for myself. At the beginning, my mission was based largely on what others had said a teacher should do. Now I am driven daily by the quest to help all students learn.

High school English teacher Carol Jago (2000) is on a mission also: to gain converts for the cause of literacy. She explains in the following:

> I suppose the fourteen years I spent in Catholic schools may have something to do with this, but I see it as my mission in life to turn students into readers whose way of moving in the world is somehow shaped by classical literature. I want them to see their own lives as a hero's journey and to have learned from Odysseus and Bilbo Baggins that even when there seems to be no hope for survival, help will appear, though not always in the shape one might expect. (pp. 68-69)

Tessa Lamb is a first-year teacher in British Columbia. She knows what it's like to work in a job "with a ceiling," and is now delighted to have a career with a calling. She was frustrated with the limitations of her former job and longed for a place where she could make a difference. She is midway through her first year and is energized by teaching.

> As I look to the future, my goal is to be able to maintain the same excitement and inspiration about teaching that I have now. I want to continue to feel the same wonder at observing children's growth and successes.

A Job With a Ceiling or a Career With a Calling?

> *Many of us became teachers for reasons of the heart, animated by a passion for some subject and for helping people learn.*
>
> Palmer (1998, p. 17)

Would you place Trait 1 at the top of your list of 10 traits? Without a mission and a calling, teaching is just another job—and a tough one at that. Jan Palfenier, an experienced upper-grade teacher, believes that a calling to teach and a passion to meet students' needs are essential to help teachers survive and get through what she calls the "burnout stage"—that period in a teacher's career when too many meetings, too little time, and parents who don't care can sap a teacher's energy. In the face of obstacles such as these, the passionate teacher "refuses to submit to apathy or cynicism" (Fried, 1995, p. 1), but clings to what Herbert Kohl (1984) calls altruism—that deep desire to serve others.

Trait 2: Positive and Real

The highly effective teacher is positive and real, demonstrating the qualities of respect, caring, empathy, and fairness in his or her communications and relationships with students, parents, and colleagues.

> All in all, the evidence seems quite clear when it comes to describing good or effective teachers on the basis of personal characteristics. Effective teachers appear to be those who are, shall

we say, "human" in the fullest sense of the word. They have a sense of humor, are fair, empathetic, more democratic than autocratic, and apparently can relate easily and naturally to students on either a one-to-one or group basis. Their classrooms seem to reflect miniature enterprise operations in the sense that they are open, spontaneous, and adaptable to change. (Hamachek, 1999, p. 212)

I am often a guest on radio call-in shows as an "education consultant." People (usually parents) phone in questions about their school concerns and I dispense advice. The program host and I typically sit in a studio with headphones and microphones while a call-screener and producer work in an adjoining room, separated from the studio by a large window. Although we can see one another, we usually communicate via a computer screen so that we know who the next caller is and what that caller's question or concern might be. During one particular program, however, the producer left her cubicle and dashed out into the studio.

"I've got one of your former students on the line," she exclaimed excitedly. I could tell this was going to make her programming day. A golden moment in broadcasting, no doubt.

"She's calling from Kansas City and wants to tell the listening audience what kind of a teacher you were."

My heart did a few flip-flops. "What's her name?" I asked.

"Melody," the producer said.

"She was in my fifth grade class in the early sixties," I said, immediately adding a last name to go with her first.

"You actually remember her?" the producer asked somewhat incredulously. Obviously, she had never been a teacher.

"Find out what she's going to say," I said, "before you put her on live." I was supposed to be giving advice, not participating in a "This Is Your Life—Elaine McEwan."

My teaching career flashed in front of me. Would Melody remember that I was a great writing teacher? We were doing process writing back in the 1960s. Would she fondly recall the fascinating novels I read aloud every day after lunch? I was into literature-based instruction before it was trendy. Perhaps the intriguing (albeit far too ambitious) interdisciplinary unit on Cultures of the Western World was indelibly etched in her mind. I had the script all written before Melody uttered a sound.

When I heard her opening words through my headset, I knew she wasn't going to offer a stirring testimonial to my curriculum and instructional methodologies. Melody simply said that I was a caring teacher. She reminded me that her mother had suffered a heart attack while Melody was in fifth grade—a traumatic experience for this tiny 10-year-old. I remembered it only after she related the details, but I had no recollection of this event figuring large in my objectives or plans. If Melody remembered any specific lessons from fifth grade, they weren't as important to her as the fact that I was kind to her. I empathized with her fears, gave her permission to cry, and temporarily set aside my teaching agenda to meet her personal needs. I cared. Hosford (1984) calls these kinds of personal interactions "the silent curriculum" (p. 146).

Elementary school teachers have thousands of such interactions with students during the school year (Jackson, 1968), while we can only speculate how many the average middle or high school teacher has as he or she meets with up to 150 students per day. These personal exchanges can either become the glue that bonds students and teachers together, or the sparks that ignite indifference, anger, and fear on both sides of the desk. One sarcastic statement or hostile glance from a teacher may be remembered for a student's lifetime.

The legislators who mandate tests, and the state boards of education who write the learning outcomes to be tested, may not fully appreciate that, when it comes to school success, who a teacher is can be just as important as curriculum and instruction. The individual traits that make up the character and person of the "positive and real" teacher are like pieces of a puzzle. When assembled, they reveal what Stephen Covey (1990) calls a "moral compass" (p. 95). This compass does not point north, south, east, and west, but rather to goodness, truth, justice, and authenticity. Every highly effective teacher has a moral compass and uses it daily by being respectful, caring, empathetic, and fair.

Respectful

I hope I convey these qualities [respect, empathy, caring, and fairness]. I don't see how one could spend much time in the profession if one didn't. Every day would otherwise be a bloody battle.

Carol Jago

Comedian Rodney Dangerfield has made the lack of respect he receives the trademark of his nightclub act and his frequent TV commercials. "I don't get no respect," he laments and then proceeds to detail the most outrageous examples of how his family and friends put him down. We laugh because we know it's all a big joke. However, being demeaned and disrespected is no joke—especially when it takes place in a school setting, and it's the students who are being bad-mouthed. One of my pet peeves as a principal was gossip about students and parents in the teachers' lounge. It's a sure sign of disrespect. We do not speak disparagingly of people whom we respect. Being genuinely respectful of others is the most fundamental aspect of being a "positive and real" person.

The teacher who does not offer genuine respect and affirmation to his or her students will constantly be frustrated and circumvented. If students know their teachers respect them, they work harder, take correction more readily, and are more willing to take responsibility for their actions. Lack of respect takes many forms—arrogance, self-centeredness, sarcasm, cynicism, and cruelty are just a few.

Even small and seemingly insignificant behaviors like remembering a student's name and giving it the correct pronunciation (i.e., the pronunciation the family uses) or greeting students and parents with warmth and genuineness in ways that are culturally appropriate are indications of respect for others. When I was a central-office administrator I was frequently invited to attend special events at each of the schools. I particularly remember one awards assembly in which many of the winners had Spanish names. The principal, who had been working with these students for a number of years, was unable to pronounce a single name correctly. I can only imagine how these students and their parents felt at this blatant lack of respect. The message his actions sent was unmistakable and reprehensible—these students and parents are not worthy of my time and effort.

Here is how one immigrant student described what lack of respect felt like for her: "I just sat in my classroom and didn't understand anything. . . . My teachers never called on me or talked to me. I think they either forgot I was there or else wished I wasn't" (Olsen, 1988, p. 49). The most profound indicator of lack of respect is total disregard. The need to feel respected and included is a fundamental human need. It must be met before any other interpersonal needs can be met.

Caring

The teacher who succeeds in getting herself [himself] loved by the pupils will obtain results which one of a more forbidding temperament finds it impossible to secure.

Henry James (1902, p. 45)

Maybe "love" made the teacher's world go round in 1902, but the operative word at the turn of this new century is "caring."

[Caring] has found its way into the language of every facet of the profession. It is being regarded as the essential ingredient for excellence in instruction, classroom management, classroom and school climate, student motivation, administrative leadership, and parent and community support systems. It pervades the educationese of the nineties. It is the theme to which a multitude of new books on education and teaching, and entire educational journals are devoted. (Agne, 1999, p. 165)

In a study of at-risk students' perception of teacher effectiveness, 47 young adults, who had either graduated or dropped out of high school, were interviewed regarding the characteristics of their teachers. A researcher asked one young woman what she would change about her school experience so that she could have been more successful as a student. Her answer is compelling. "Actually, having teachers care. I saw a lot of teachers there to be there. To be making money. They really didn't care. Some teachers did, but some teachers just didn't care" (Peart & Campbell, 1999, p. 272). Teachers who were identified by students as changing their lives were rarely praised for their knowledge of subject matter, teaching methods, or materials. Those were all givens in their students' minds. What really mattered to students were the teachers' human qualities (Coppedge & Shreck, 1988).

Carl Rogers, the eminent psychotherapist, was fascinated with the relationship between what he called the facilitative conditions (e.g., understanding, caring, and genuineness) and learning in the classroom (Rogers, 1957). He hypothesized that students would learn more and behave better if they were taught by high-facilitative teachers (i.e., individuals with high levels of understanding, caring, and genuineness) as compared to students taught by low-facilitative teachers. Aspy and Roebuck (1977) tested Rogers's hypothesis in a variety of classroom and school studies. They reported their findings in a book, the title of which should be emblazoned on the walls of all of the teachers' lounges in America: *Kids Don't Learn From People They Don't Like* (1977). The studies described the students of high-facilitative teachers, those individuals who are empathetic, genuine, and have respect for students. These students were found to make greater gains on academic achievement measures, including both math and reading scores and present fewer disciplinary problems (Aspy & Roebuck, 1977, p. 46).

Many teachers believe that if they care too much about students they will jeopardize the dominant-subordinate relationships they need to maintain order in their classrooms. They rarely allow students to see them as warm and caring, fearful of the consequences. Highly effective teachers, by contrast, recognize and manage the tension between caring and control. They know that "warmth without control is not warmth at all but chaos and confusion, and control without warmth is not control but tyranny" (Borich, 1993, p. 124).

Empathetic

Empathy is the key to influence.

Covey (1990, p. 149)

A keen ability to sense what was happening in another person's inner world enabled Linda Taylor, the special education teacher of whom you read in Chapter 1, to teach one of her students to read. Robert was hostile, uncommunicative, angry, and often violent when he arrived in Linda's classroom as a freshman. He was also illiterate. One could never have guessed from observing Robert at his high school graduation that four years earlier he was one of his district's most troubled students. Then he held the record for "most classes attended and suspended from by a behavior-disordered student under the age of 14." Robert specialized in getting booted from schools taught by teachers who specialized in teaching students like Robert. He tangled with the best and won. What was responsible for turning around Robert's behavior almost overnight? He learned to read! Who was responsible for making it happen? A gifted teacher who asked only one question, "Why does Robert act the way he does?" Linda understood Robert's hellish inner world, the despair and frustration he felt when teachers ignored his inability to read and focused solely on his behavior.

On the auspicious day when Linda met Robert for the first time, she was able to communicate an understanding and depth of feeling for his plight that he had never before felt from a teacher. Linda promised Robert that if he would stick with her, she would teach him to read. Robert graduated in June 2001, reading at a middle-school level, having made more than seven years of progress in only four years of instruction.

I recently had the privilege of introducing Robert to more than 100 principals and teachers, participants in one of my workshops on raising reading achievement. I asked him what advice he would give these educators regarding how to do a better job of reaching their at-risk students. Robert spoke succinctly but eloquently to the group. "You should get to know your students as individuals. Before Mrs. Taylor, no one knew I couldn't read." We know better, of course. Robert's reading level and testing results were part of his voluminous case file. We understand that plenty of teachers knew that Robert couldn't read. They just didn't care. They had been hired to change his behavior, not teach him to read. They were focused on control, not caring.

> The love of nurturing and observing growth in others is essential to sustaining a life of teaching. This implies that no matter what you teach or how you present yourself to your students, you have to be on the learner's side and to believe that they can and will grow during the time that you are together. (Kohl, 1984, p. 5)

We know that Linda's skill as a reading teacher is unsurpassed, her command of content and methodology is superb, but where would Robert be today without her empathy, honesty, and compassion? "It is impossible to separate the person from the professional" (Sparks & Lipka, 1992, p. 310).

Fair

> *Students can tolerate many conditions in the classroom, but injustice is an area that creates conflict between teacher and students. Calling on the same students; smiling, praising and giving rewards to only a select few in the classroom; believing one student over another in a dispute;*

*and using the same students for leadership positions in the class are a
few examples of what students feel are unfair.*

                    Houston, Clift, Freibert, & Warner (1988, p. 234)

There are dozens of ways in which teachers demonstrate their fairness or lack thereof: how they choose teams, how they decide who was at fault in an argument or classroom dispute, how they choose helpers, how they hand out classroom perks, how they hand out positive comments and praise, and in how they pay attention to students. One at-risk adolescent put it this way:

We should get equal attention, but they [the teachers], make no effort. They focus on the good kids, they don't reach out. My math teacher treats me like dirt. I'm either embarrassed or ignored. I was told in front of the whole class that I failed my test. (Taylor-Dunlop & Norton, 1997, p. 276)

Students will make allowances for many teacher mistakes or character flaws, but unfairness or partiality is rarely forgiven or forgotten. Highly effective teachers cultivate fairness intentionally and thoughtfully, knowing its importance to both students and their parents.

The Positive and Real Teacher

*You can teach without empathy and understanding, but will the
students learn?*

                                            Marsha Arest

Think about the people with whom you like to spend your time. They are the individuals who build you up; affirm your strengths; understand your problems; respect your unique qualities; and tell you the truth in love. They are positive and real. Would you rather take instruction, direction, and correction from someone like that, or from someone who is critical, angry, hostile, cold, unfriendly, and self-centered? Who do you think will make the most effective teacher? Our students deserve teachers that are positive and real.

Trait 3: A Teacher-Leader

The highly effective teacher is a "teacher-leader" who positively affects the lives of students, parents, and colleagues.

> *Teaching and leading are clearly distinguishable occupations, but every great leader is clearly teaching—and every great teacher is leading.*
>
> Gardner (1989, p. 18)

Leadership is influencing others to change, learn, grow, expand, move forward, do things differently, become independent, take responsibility, and achieve goals. Highly effective teachers wield this influence in three very different, but highly connected arenas: the classroom, the school, and the community. The teaching profession, by its very nature, militates against the concept of teacher-leaders. Lieberman (1988) describes the "egalitarian ethic" that almost mandates teachers to think of everyone as the same, no matter "how experienced, how effective or how knowledgeable" individual teachers may be (p. 7). Yet, the sense of mission and passion for making a difference that drives highly effective teachers will not find its full expression until they are able to step forward and assume leadership roles.

Some teachers, however, have a difficult time seeing themselves in leadership roles.

> Teaching is not a profession that values or encourages leadership within its ranks. The hierarchical nature of public schools is based on the 19th-century industrial model, with the consequent adversarial relationship of administration as management and teachers as labor. (Troen & Boles, 1994, p. 40)

Some teachers feel that the principal is in charge and teachers merely follow orders. They feel uncomfortable with making decisions and taking responsibility, believing that those are administrative prerogatives. However, the individual who sees teaching as anything other than an opportunity to lead, misses the mark completely. The highly effective teacher provides leadership to students, parents, and colleagues.

Leading Students

While listening with an open heart and mind, [teachers] must try to lead their students to see and understand things afresh.

Banner & Cannon (1997, p. 42)

If one can successfully lead in the classroom, one can lead anywhere. After all, students are not employees. We have no binding legal contracts with them. They receive no financial rewards for their hard work. "The joy of learning is its own reward," we tell our students. Yet we expect them to be on the job for more than five hours every day, be responsible for working after hours, have little or no input with regard to working conditions, and still be cheerful, obedient, and trustworthy. Can you imagine a more challenging leadership role than this? Highly effective teachers provide leadership in their classrooms in five important ways:

1. Through example

2. Through listening

3. Through empowering

4. Through inspiration

5. Through learning

Leadership Through Example

The teacher who meets with the most success is the teacher whose own ways are the most imitable. (Henry James, 1902, p. 49)

Much of a teacher's leading is done by example. Teachers model life-long learning when they share their personal interests and talk about books they have read or ideas that intrigue them. Teachers model kindness and patience when they show their students how to respond to anger and hostility with equanimity. Teachers model how to read and write when they think aloud and explain the strategies they are using. Teachers model social skills when they are courteous and respectful to their students, colleagues, and parents. Sometimes teachers do their most powerful leading when not a word is spoken. "Every action we take affects us and those around us. We are like dominoes. When we move, we cause others to move. . . . Many times we are communicating most loudly when we say nothing" (Munson, 1991, pp. 45-46).

We are currently engaged in a massive undertaking in the public schools—"teaching" character to our students in the hopes that worksheets, slogans, and banners will somehow infuse them with kindness and honesty. Meanwhile the same teachers who have preached patience during the character lessons can be overheard in the school office screaming at the secretary because she didn't deliver a message or complete their photocopying request. Teachers are teaching honesty during character classes while coming late and leaving early. Teachers bemoan their students' lack of respect for one another, but think nothing of putting down parents or berating colleagues. The moral dimensions of the relationship between teacher and students demand leadership by example. "Children desperately need adults to look up to, adults from whom they can learn by experience what it means to confirm another, to honor another, and to respect self and others" (Burke & Nierenberg, 1998, p. 341). Highly effective teachers lead by example and are the role models that young people need.

Leadership Through Listening

Teachers are so verbal. They lecture, guide, and coach. But great teaching also involves effective listening. Listening to students' questions and concerns, listening for misunderstandings, and listening to that which goes unsaid. Of all the communication skills, perhaps listening is the most important.

Marsha Arest

Teachers are talkers. An individual would not likely choose a teaching career, if that individual did not like to talk. Highly effective teachers, however, know when to stop talking and start listening. They are masters of what I call "wordless advice." Good teachers are able to suspend "teacher talk" and let their students learn while talking about what they are thinking or through verbalizing their feelings or problems. Steve Linhardt finds that "[through listening] I find out about my students and see how they handle adversity, struggles, and successes. I can share with them in their accomplishments and their disappointments." Often the most powerful insights regarding the problems of learning and life come when a student is able to think aloud to a compassionate teacher. This leadership role, though unseen and unspectacular, is one that highly effective teachers exercise regularly.

Leadership Through Empowering

Highly effective teachers know that it is only when students are empowered to take charge of their own learning that a teacher's true mission has been accomplished. Meichenbaum and Biemiller (1998) call it nurturing independent learners. They describe a process of student goal setting that makes students "much more likely to engage in deliberate practice, to intentionally plan and self-monitor their performance, and to persist in the face of failure and frustration" (p. 148). Teacher-leaders nurture goal setting and help students understand how the achievement of a goal will bring added value to their lives (e.g., once you learn to read on your own, you won't have to wait for someone to read aloud to you; or once you are able to write well, you won't have to worry about completing essays for job or college applications). Teacher-leaders ask students to reflect on their learning by regularly asking them to write responses to questions like these: (a) When can you use what you learned today? (b) What did you like best (or least) about today's class? (c) What do you know you know? (Meichenbaum & Biemiller, 1998).

Teachers also empower students by giving them ownership and control over what happens in the classroom. Marsha Arest, a Spanish teacher at Blind Brook High School in Rye, New York, empowers her students by means of a classroom contract, negotiated at the beginning of the school year. Marsha explains: "The contract contains mutually agreed upon curriculum goals, teacher and student responsibilities, and assessment procedures" According to Marsha, the contract she has with her students differs from most legal contracts in one significant way: "Our contract is a *living* document that is constantly being renegotiated as we encounter problems that we cannot solve under the current contract language."

Leadership Through Inspiration

Teachers must inspire as well as instruct.
> Words carved in limestone at the entrance to the
> School of Education on the University of Indiana campus

Leadership by inspiration involves a deeply interpersonal dimension in which teachers and students connect with one another. Teachers who lead by inspiration leave a lasting and profound impression on their students.

> These are the teachers who help children find their own competence through success at meeting challenges. . . . These are the teachers who illuminate the unique gifts and talents that are present in each child. And, these are the teachers who inspire children to take risks academically, socially, and emotionally. (Burke & Nierenberg, 1998, p. 351)

To inspire is to enliven and encourage—to stimulate and to activate latent talents and creativity. To inspire is to bring forth achievement from discouragement and despair, to bring forth confidence from frustration and failure.

Leadership Through Learning

The ability to inspire and motivate students is facilitated when teacher-leaders are willing to seek input from their students (and the students' parents) regarding their teaching effectiveness. Excellent teachers realize that their pupils possess a great deal of information about teachers' teaching effectiveness, and the teachers are willing to take the risks inherent in soliciting that input—opening themselves to their students' honest appraisals. Asking their students to give input regarding their instructional strengths and weaknesses is the ultimate sign of respect from teacher to student. If done in forthright and transparent ways, the process holds the promise of strengthening teacher–student bonds and forging a "mutually supportive, symbiotic relationship" (Pellicer & Anderson, 1995, p. 130).

Leading Parents

> *Building relationships with students and families is a priority for me—both at school and beyond the classroom doors. I always give out my home phone number and my email address so that if there is a problem, parents can contact me anytime. I'm visible at sports, music, and dance events so I can bond with families. I speak from my heart so that parents will feel my genuine affection for their child.*
>
> Adrienne Hamparian Johnson

The idea that teachers should play a leadership role where parents are concerned may be a new one for many educators. Perhaps the phrase "parent involvement" sounds more familiar, but how better to involve parents in the education of their students than by leading them? Many parents seem to know intuitively how to be involved, but others need strong teacher leadership. Highly effective teachers know how to provide the kind of leadership that brings parents into an active partnership with teachers. Outstanding teachers provide leadership to parents through (a) affirmation, (b) collaboration, (c) invitation, (d) communication, and (e) information.

Consider just a few examples of how outstanding teachers provide leadership to parents.

- Teachers lead through affirmation by making positive phone calls and writing positive notes to parents about their children.

- Teachers lead through collaboration by asking parents for observations on their child's homework activities (e.g., difficulties, limitations, what went well).

- Teachers lead through invitation by asking parents to evaluate their teaching practices, the assignments they give to students, and their homework policies.

- Teachers lead through communication by providing parents with a written general description of what will be covered during the school year and a brief explanation of why these activities are important.

- Teachers lead through information by providing parents with an ongoing assignment calendar of the work that will be covered in class and why this work is important.

Leading Colleagues

In . . . good schools the image is one of teachers with voice and vision. Teachers are knowledgeable and discerning school actors who are the primary shapers of the educational environment.

Lightfoot (1985, p. 24)

A highly effective teacher exhibits leadership skills not only with students and parents, but also among colleagues. There are numerous ways that all teachers, even newcomers, can be leaders of their colleagues:

1. Mentoring and coaching novice teachers

2. Collaborating with all staff members regardless of personal affiliation or preference

3. Learning and growing with a view to bringing new ideas to the classroom and school

4. Polishing writing and presentation skills to share knowledge with others

5. Engaging in creative problem solving and decision making with increased student learning as the goal

6. Being willing to take risks in front of peers

7. Being willing to share ideas, opinions, and evaluative judgments confidently with the principal (McEwan, 1998b, p. 101)

Leadership among colleagues is as much about teamwork as it is about being out in front leading the charge. Highly effective teachers are team players. "They have conquered their egos. For them schools are too important to use as personal battlegrounds for bolstering themselves at the expense of students, colleagues, parents, and administrators" (Borich, 1993, p. 120).

A Person of Influence

A leader is a "person who is in a position to influence others to act and who has, as well, the moral, intellectual, and social skills required to take advantage of that position" (Schlechty, 1990, p. xix). Who is that person? A highly effective teacher, of course. No other group of individuals wields as much leadership power over as many people as teachers do. Highly effective teachers possess the moral, intellectual, and social skills to use their leadership for good in the lives of students, parents, and colleagues.

Recapping Chapter 2

Chapter 2 has described the personal traits that signify character in the highly effective teacher. Through the discussion and examples in this chapter we have discovered that the highly effective teacher is a multi-faceted individual—a positive and real person, someone who is mission-driven and passionate regarding teaching, as well as a leader who is willing to take risks for the opportunity to make a difference in the lives of students, parents, and colleagues. Figure 2.1, Personal Traits That Signify Character, graphically summarizes the personal traits.

Looking Ahead

Being a person of quality and character doesn't automatically confer the mantle of master teacher upon an individual. The ability to teach is essential as well. I concur with Saphier and Gower (1967), who say,

> We do not mean to imply that being skillful substitutes for other human qualities; but we will argue that whatever else teachers do, they perform in the classroom and their actions set the stage for students' experiences—therefore, only a skillful performance will do. (p. v)

In Chapters 3, 4, and 5, we will examine the four teaching traits that get results and specifically target what it is that highly effective teachers do during teaching that results in learning and student achievement.

Figure 2.1. Personal Traits That Signify Character: What an Effective Teacher *Is*

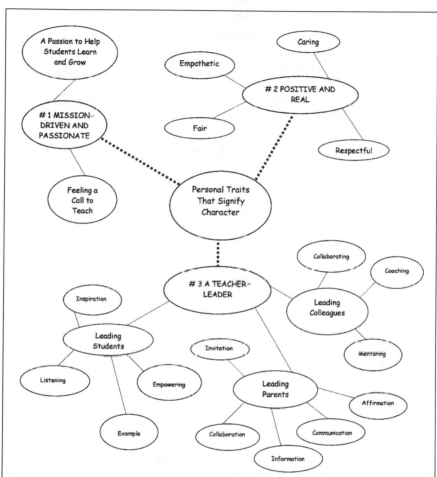

3

Teaching Traits That Get Results

With-It-Ness and Style

The essence of being an effective teacher lies in knowing what to do to foster pupils' learning and being able to do it.

Kyriacou (1991, p. 1)

A s a brand-new elementary school principal in the early 1980s, I was immediately faced with the devastating fallout of ineffective teaching. Achievement was at the 20th percentile in reading and mathematics and although the school's demographics might have dictated such a state of affairs to some observers, there were clearly other variables at work as well. I came to think of one of these variables as my own "Bermuda Triangle." Much as ships and planes disappear into the mythical Bermuda Triangle, large numbers of students at Lincoln School disappeared into an academic and behavioral Bermuda Triangle. Oh, there were many effective teachers to be sure, but their effect was diluted by the presence of the ineffective ones. This depressing state of affairs was further exacerbated by a system of tracking in which the most at-risk students were often placed with the most inept instructors, creating further behavioral and academic declines. Many students were doomed to failure from the moment they enrolled. The effective teachers were demoralized, weary of trying to compensate for the miserable classroom management and insipid instruction perpetrated by their colleagues.

During my first two years as a principal, I put in endless cycles of observing, documenting, conferencing, and remediating. I was appalled by the anger, hostility, and disrespect for students; the almost nonexistent instruction; and by the total disregard for district curriculum standards that I found in the classrooms of ineffective teachers. With the support of my superintendent, the school board, and an excellent attorney, the tide began to turn. We were no longer drowning, just treading water like crazy. Test scores went up. My heightened expectations for both students and teachers, together with a dismissal or two, began to have an effect, not only on the average teachers who decided it might be a good time to improve their teaching skills, but also on the many outstanding teachers. The highly effective ones began to emerge from their classrooms and talk with one another about instruction. It was once again popular to be "a good teacher." Test scores continued to rise.

In subsequent years we organized peer-coaching opportunities, videotaped lessons so that teachers could view and reflect on their own teaching, and formed grade-level teams to develop learning outcomes for students. We brought in experts to challenge us and read the research literature on effective teaching voraciously. We were constantly about the business of improving instruction—implementing direct instruction to bring our lowest achieving students up to grade level in basic skills, as well as cooperative learning, cognitive strategy instruction, and hands-on learning in every classroom. We varied our teaching approaches to meet the diverse needs of our students. At the end of eight years, our scores were near the 80th percentile. Highly effective teachers made it happen; they threw lifelines of learning to students who were drowning in despair and defeat. They taught them what they needed to know to be successful in school.

The teaching traits of highly effective teachers are central and absolutely essential to students' learning. These are the traits that have the power to get results: with-it-ness, style, motivational expertise, and instructional effectiveness. We will examine with-it-ness and style in this chapter, look at motivational expertise in Chapter 4, and consider instructional effectiveness in Chapter 5.

Trait 4: With-It-Ness

The highly effective teacher demonstrates with-it-ness: the state of being on top of, tuned in to, aware of, and in complete control of three critical facets of classroom life:

1. The management and organization of the classroom

2. The engagement of students

3. The management of time

> The novice [as well as the master] teacher must be attentive to everything, even to the most innocent movements on the part of the students: the restlessness of their bodies, a surprised gaze, or a more or less aggressive reaction on the part of this or that student. (Freire, 1998, p. 49)

Jacob Kounin coined the very descriptive term *with-it-ness* (1970, p. 74). The word reminds me of the proverbial eyes in the back of her head that my mother assured us she had. When my brother and I were small, it was not difficult for us to believe that this was indeed true. Although we could not see my mother's second set of eyes, she always seemed to know when we were doing something naughty. It didn't matter that she was in another room. If we stuck out our tongues at each other, she would call from the kitchen in an all-knowing way, "I saw that. Stop it, right now." We would look at each other in awe at her omniscience.

My mother also had another characteristic that Kounin includes in his description of with-it-ness, called "overlappingness." This is the uncanny ability to do seven things at the same time. My mother could talk on the phone, peel potatoes, tie a shoelace, and wipe a dirty face—all without missing a beat. Highly effective teachers are masters of multitasking, just like my mother. They can teach, walk around the classroom, take in everything that's going on, and signal off-task students all without missing a beat. Ineffective teachers, by contrast, can scarcely manage starting a lesson on time. "With-it-ness requires the ability to simultaneously attend to a variety of stimuli and then to appropriately categorize what is observed and quickly respond in a way that will prevent disruption and maintain the flow of the lesson" (Bullough, 1989, p. 47).

My definition of with-it-ness encompasses more than just omni-science and multitasking, however. With-it-ness in the context of our discussion includes being on top of, tuned in to, and aware of everything that is happening in the classroom, and then being able to handle it, manage it, and react to it, in efficient and effective ways to promote student learning.

There are three areas of classroom life in which highly effective teachers display their awesome powers of with-it-ness:

1. Classroom organization and management

2. Engagement of students

3. The effective use of time

Figure 3.1 provides a graphic organizer to help you preview the many aspects of with-it-ness.

Classroom Organization and Management

The ability to organize and manage a classroom should be the cornerstone of any College of Education curriculum.

Janice Palfenier

Classroom management is a set of behaviors and activities by which the teacher organizes and maintains classroom conditions that bring about effective and efficient instruction. I have always compared classroom management to the plumbing and electrical systems in a house. When the toilets and the lights are working, no one even thinks about them. They are just there doing what they were intended to do. When the toilets won't flush and the house is in the dark, however, a state of emergency is declared until services can be restored. In well-managed classrooms where procedures, schedules, expectations, and routines have been taught, modeled, practiced, and reinforced, teaching looks effortless. The naïve observer thinks to himself or herself, "I could do this. Teaching is really no big deal." The highly effective teacher just smiles. "Of course you could. If you knew what I know and could do what I've done." What this highly effective teacher has done is to develop a set of procedures that "demonstrate how people are to function in an acceptable and organized manner" (Wong & Wong, 1998, p. 172). This is no

Figure 3.1. Trait 4: With-It-Ness

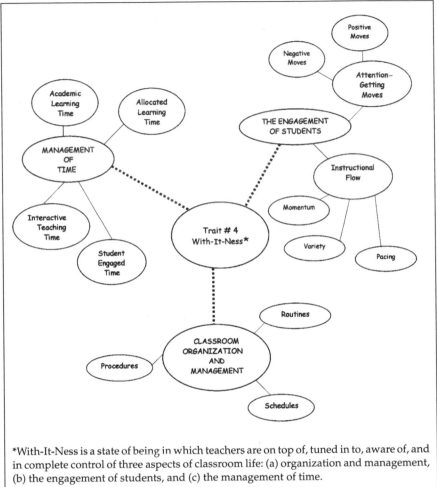

*With-It-Ness is a state of being in which teachers are on top of, tuned in to, aware of, and in complete control of three aspects of classroom life: (a) organization and management, (b) the engagement of students, and (c) the management of time.

small achievement. Without order, opportunities for learning are diminished, if not totally undermined.

Donna Garner, a high school English and Spanish teacher in Texas, believes that her classroom organizational skills help her lay the foundation for a successful school year.

The parameters must be set in place meticulously at the beginning of the year so that all students know where the boundaries are. Students feel more secure in such a setting and can concentrate better. We may get somewhat loud during the period while working with partners or doing other activities, but we always begin and end the period with focused control.

Highly effective teachers have well-managed and well-organized classrooms.

The Engagement of Students

How can a teacher (or other observer) tell if students are engaged? It's pretty obvious. For one thing, they act involved. They are reading, writing, taking notes, manipulating materials, doing experiments, drawing diagrams, answering questions, asking questions, listening, using a computer or calculator, interacting in small groups with their fellow students, or talking with the teacher. They also look involved. Their eyes follow the teacher as the teacher moves about the room; they are alert, energetic, and even their posture and body language suggest engagement. There might even be a palpable sense of excitement in a classroom when students are engaged. How do highly skilled teachers keep students engaged? There are two ways: (a) through instructional flow and (b) through attention-getting moves.

Instructional Flow

We have all attended workshops in which time literally flies. We look at our watches and lunch is just around the corner. "Where did the morning go?" we wonder. There are other occasions during which the minutes drag by. Our minds wander and our eyelids grow heavy. There are numerous variables that affect attention, of course, many of them beyond any presenter or teacher's control. Three variables, however, when skillfully manipulated, make even reluctant attendees or students sit up and take notice:

1. Variety

2. Momentum

3. Pacing

They compose the essence of instructional flow.

Variety. "Variety's the very spice of life," the saying goes (Cowper, 1785/1968). It is also the spice of classroom life. Just as kitchen spices must be used judiciously, classroom variety must be judiciously and sparingly applied during the school day. Highly effective teachers focus on achievement, not merely on "activities," but they also recognize the truth of another old saying: "All work and no play [or variety] makes Jack a dull boy" (Howell, 1659/1992).

Highly effective teachers use a variety of teaching approaches (e.g., direct instruction, role-playing, inquiry, discovery learning, or simulations); a variety of assignments and assessments (e.g., portfolios, quizzes, projects, or essays); a variety of attention-getting moves (e.g., alerting, desisting, and enlisting); a variety of grouping practices (e.g., small skill groups, whole groups, cooperative groups, competitive classroom teams); a variety of technological enhancements (e.g., overheads, computers, videos, or calculators); and a variety of seating arrangements (e.g., circles, clusters, rows, or pairs). Highly effective teachers are consistent and predictable in many important ways: they are always fair, always on-task, always respectful, always organized, always focused on a specific learning outcome, and always upbeat. However, they are quite unpredictable with regard to the ways that they seek to keep their students engaged. Highly effective teachers know they must match the variety they encounter in the classroom with variety of their own creation.

Momentum. Variety is not the only way that skillful teachers keep students engaged. They also use momentum to keep the instructional wagon moving westward. They do this in the following ways:

- *They are always prepared.* Highly effective teachers have their supplies, materials, and equipment prepared before the day begins. They do not interrupt instructional flow to find the right book or to get more photocopies made.

- *They are tuned in.* Skillful teachers are constantly tuned in to their students looking for confusion, lack of understanding, inability to move on to the next task, or complete off-task behavior. They are scanning the radar, as it were, constantly on the lookout for blips on the screen that indicate the potential for losing a student's attention or the possibility of a disciplinary problem.

- *They are indistractible.* Outstanding teachers are able to manage seemingly countless intrusions and distractions to their own trains of thought without disrupting the instructional flow for students.

- *They are flexible.* Master teachers maintain flexibility with regard to their lessons or planned activities and can change direction immediately if necessary. They are never locked into a plan that is not working.

- *They have a built-in early warning system.* Highly effective teachers understand that students need brief updates or reminders about transitions and advance notice of unexpected changes during the school day. They use them to keep students on track and on-task.

- *They are mind readers.* Highly effective teachers anticipate, predict, and even seem to read minds. Highly effective teachers are rarely caught off guard by unexpected happenings in the classroom.

- *They are good at crowd control.* The best teachers are able to direct the movement of small groups of students around their classrooms with a minimum of fuss and time loss as well as taking whole groups to assemblies or on field trips. Their students move quietly, quickly, and without undue intervention from the teacher.

Pacing. Pacing is the third and final way in which highly effective teachers keep instruction flowing and students engaged. Pacing has to do with the speed at which a teacher moves through a lesson or instructional sequence. Ineffective teachers have no pattern at all to their pacing, while highly effective teachers vary their pacing to match the individuals or groups with whom they are working. What would be an unbearably slow pace for one group of students working on a particular objective might be perfect for another. The highly effective teacher makes the necessary adjustments to keep all students engaged and learning.

Highly effective teachers always plan instruction with the goal of engaging all students, but they are realistic enough to know that many students need more than good intentions or even well-planned lessons to keep them on-task. From time to time, many students, even the best ones, need a move from the teacher to bring them back from daydreaming, worrying, or just plain troublemaking. Skillful teachers, in addition to monitoring instructional flow, have a variety of attention-getting moves to recapture the waning or lost attention of students.

Attention-Getting Moves

The teacher, following out his customary role, attempts to delimit the social interaction of the classroom. . . . Thus the teacher continually strives to evoke in students the attitudinal set which we call "attention." . . . The attention of the students tends to wander from the cut-and-dried subject matter. As attention wanders, the scope of social interaction broadens. The teacher brings it back in a manner very similar to that of a dog driving a herd of sheep.

Waller (1932, p. 333)

In this quotation, Waller compares a teacher trying to keep the attention of a class of students to "a dog driving a herd of sheep," and the analogy is an apt one. The highly effective teacher is constantly on the move, nipping and barking at the heels of the students who may be fooling around, daydreaming, socializing, playing with their pens, or distracting their classmates. There are, in fact, several categories of attention moves that successful teachers use to engage their students: (a) desisting, (b) alerting, (c) enlisting, (d) acknowledging, and (e) winning (Saphier & Gower, 1997). Without the students' attention, the best-planned and well-executed lesson is taught for naught.

Even in the most well-organized and masterfully managed classrooms, students manage to slip away. The skillful teacher recognizes the slippage almost before it happens and knows just the right moves to bring an individual student or the entire class back to task. In their compendium of teaching skills, *The Skillful Teacher,* Saphier and Gower (1997) list over 50 different attention-getting moves in five different categories.

Desisting Moves. Desisting moves are the hardest to ignore. They communicate to students the need to stop what they are doing and do something else. Desisting moves can punish, warn, or reprimand, or they can be subtle physical moves like moving closer to a student's seat or gently touching a student's desk. There are also more neutral desisting moves designed to get everyone's attention at once such as the use of a xylophone or the clapping of hands in rhythm. The message is unmistakable, however: Pay attention!

Alerting Moves. Alerting moves are intended to get or keep the attention of the group as a whole. The teacher does not target a specific student but rather engages in actions or behaviors that get everyone's attention, such as making eye contact with as many students as possible, asking for responses in unison, calling on students in random order, or startling students by suddenly turning off the overhead projector or the VCR.

Enlisting Moves. Enlisting moves are less authoritarian in nature and often rely on the teacher's enthusiasm and style to draw a wandering student back to attending. They include moves like varying the tone of voice (e.g., whispering), arousing students' curiosity, or encouraging the class to imagine or fantasize. These more dramatic ways of gaining attention do not carry the negative baggage of desisting moves.

Acknowledging Moves. Even the most motivated and on-task students can be distracted by worries, problems, or other priorities. They respond best to acknowledging moves—private words from the teacher to let them know: "I understand that you are distracted today, but try to pay attention while I explain this problem."

Winning Moves. The last category of attention moves is called winning and relies on the sheer force of the teacher's interpersonal skills to "win over" a reluctant student. Outstanding teachers use winning moves whenever possible, while less-effective teachers rely on negative moves like punishment, exclusion, threats, sarcasm, and reprimands.

The Effective Use of Time

> *I believe in utilizing every single minute of class time. I treat each minute like a valuable gold coin.*
>
> Donna Garner

The effective use of time is the third and final aspect of with-it-ness, Trait 4. When I talk to educators about the critical importance of using time wisely, I humorously suggest there are two kinds of teachers. The first is like a retired senior citizen at the wheel of an RV; the second is similar to an over-the-road truck driver. The senior driver has all the time in the world, may or may not have a specific destination or deadline, and can meander at will to check out antique stores or little-known historical sites. The long-distance driver, by contrast, has places to go and things to do. Stops for fuel and food are limited and carefully timed.

Many teachers approach their long-term learning goals like the RV driver. They are in no hurry and are willing to be distracted by anyone at any time. Highly effective teachers, conversely, teach like over-the-road truckers drive. They are constantly aware of where they need to be and make every minute in their journey count. Donna Garner is the quintessential "trucker teacher." Her high school English students carry their writing utensils in a plastic zipper bag so they will always have their pens and pencils handy. That simple organizational trick might sound like overkill, but Donna explains:

> We move back and forth from one writing instrument to another very quickly. My students are required to organize their notebooks and textbooks as well. I don't want to waste a single minute with students scrambling around trying to locate materials.

Why worry about time? The answer is commonsensical enough, but it is also supported by a large body of research: the more time students spend on learning, the more they will learn (Anderson, 1975; Bloom, 1974; Fisher et al., 1978; Rim & Coller, 1982). There are several kinds of time in school. For learning to occur, they must all be present:

1. Allocated learning time

2. Student engaged time

3. Academic learning time

4. Interactive instruction (Saphier & Gower, 1997, p. 64)

Most educators are familiar with the idea of allocated learning time. It is the amount of time set aside to teach a given subject every day (or weekly). Allocated learning time is a necessary, but insufficient prerequisite for achievement, however, because there is a big difference in how individual teachers and students make use of the time allocated for a specific subject.

A second crucial measure of the degree to which students have the opportunity to learn is the amount of time students are actually attending to what is being taught. This is called student engaged time. Students are engaged when they are working on assignments or attending to the teacher. There is one small glitch in the "engaged time" concept, however. Teachers who have a hidden curriculum—for example, a subject they like to talk about that is more interesting to them than the history or physics they were hired to teach—may be very successful at gaining their students' rapt attention, but the time is wasted as far as reaching any specified learning outcomes are concerned.

Skilled teachers recognize that even when a student seems to be attending, time slippage can be occurring, because for learning to take place, a student must be experiencing success at the assigned task. A third kind of school time, academic learning time, occurs when a student is successfully engaged in learning. The fourth and final kind of school time is interactive instruction. This is time spent in receiving direct instruction or input from the teacher, as opposed to time spent doing independent assignments or group activities.

Let's follow Jason, a typical first-grader, during the two hours allocated to reading instruction in his classroom. You may be surprised to discover how little academic learning and interactive time he actually receives. Jason spends over 20 minutes during the allocated time period silently reading a book. We cannot assume with any certainty that he is engaged at a high rate of success, however, because we cannot hear him reading. If he has not sufficiently mastered the sound-spelling correspondences needed to independently decode the words of his text, has not memorized most of them from a list of sight vocabulary, or does not understand the meanings of important words or concepts, he may only be going through the motions of reading—guessing and looking at the pictures. We can only hope that his teacher has taken all of these variables into account when providing material for Jason to read. Time spent does not count as academic learning time unless the student is experiencing a 95% success rate.

Later in the morning, Jason joins some of his classmates who are moving to various learning centers, facilitated by parent volunteers. Although Jason is clearly engaged and successful at each center, the activities he is doing (e.g., cutting, pasting, and coloring) have dubious value in terms of achieving the overall first-grade reading objective. As it happens (in all too many classrooms), Jason does not receive any interaction instruction time (i.e., time spent directly with the teacher receiving instruction) during his two hours of allocated reading time—the teacher failed to plan wisely and Jason's group won't meet until the next day. The two hours Jason spent in reading instruction on the day just described unfortunately contributed absolutely nothing to the major instructional goal of first grade: learning to read with automaticity, fluency, and understanding.

Highly effective teachers use their allocated time wisely. Their classrooms are so well organized and tightly managed that little of their allocated time is wasted on noninstructional activities. One study showed that highly effective teachers provided more than twice as much academic learning time for students as average teachers did and more than six times as much academic learning time as a group of low-average teachers provided (Caldwell, Huitt, & Graeber, 1982). Highly effective teachers spend a high percentage of their time engaged with students— they do not use class time to grade papers, make lesson plans, and do housekeeping tasks. In one study, students in classrooms where teachers had lower rates of interaction with students (i.e., below the 73% average for all teachers in the study) had significantly smaller achievement gains (or no gain at all), especially if they were low-performing students (Stallings, 1980). Highly skilled teachers are masters at determining exactly what instructional activities their students need to help them be successfully engaged in learning, whether it is remedial help for low-performing students or enrichment and acceleration for high-performing students. Highly effective teachers are rarely distracted from their goals and thus provide the maximum number of students with the opportunity to learn. To return to our highway analogy, highly effective teachers aren't parked at a scenic overlook taking photos for their albums; they are driving to their appointed destinations.

Highly effective teachers cannot make every minute count by themselves, however. They need the support of their administrators to limit the use of the school intercom and schedule uninterrupted instruction time for key mastery subjects. Highly effective teachers resent interruptions, lost time, and lack of respect for the lessons they have so carefully crafted. They would like their teaching to be accorded the same respect that teaching is accorded in Japan. There, the lesson is sacred. Highly effective teachers would like to post "Do Not Disturb" signs on their doors every day—not just during achievement testing week.

With-It or Out-of-It?

With-it was used in my era to refer to someone who was tuned in to the latest in music, fashion, and pop culture. If you were with-it you knew what was "in" and "cool." If you weren't, you were "out-of-it." Highly effective teachers are, in the popular vernacular of days gone by, with-it. They know what's happening, and what's more, they know how to respond to it. If you need to review the complexities and intricacies of with-it-ness as evidenced in (a) classroom organization and management; (b) the management of time; and (c) the engagement of students, return to Figure 3.1, found at the beginning of the chapter.

Trait 5: Style

The effective teacher exhibits his or her own unique style, bringing drama, enthusiasm, liveliness, humor, charisma, creativity, and novelty to his or her teaching.

> *The basic elements of teaching . . . are qualities that come to inhere in us, even if we do not recognize them as such or fully develop them. Rarely can they be taught. They are ingredients of our own humanity, to which contents and methods are adjunct. We must draw them from ourselves, identify, develop, and then apply them. We may know our subjects and perfect our techniques for teaching them without recognizing that, for our mastery to make a difference to our students, we must also summon from within certain qualities of personality that have little to do with subject matter or theories of instruction.*
>
> Banner & Cannon (1997, p. 2)

Style is the second of the teaching traits that get results. Figure 3.2 provides a graphic preview of the many ways in which highly effective teachers express their unique personalities. Style may seem to be a rather unimportant or even frivolous trait when compared to the other traits in this category, but it continues to emerge as one that matters a great deal to students and engages them when every other teaching trick fails. Teachers' styles don't have to be far-out or flamboyant. There are highly effective teachers who are gentle, quiet, soft, and subtle. Style, according to Webster, is "distinction, excellence, originality in any form of artistic . . . expression" (McKechnie, 1983, p. 1810).

Finding Your Own Style

I was a very ordinary fifth-grade teacher compared to my grade-level counterpart with whom I shared a classroom wall. A sweet girl graduate of the early 1960s, I dressed in matching sweater sets and

Figure 3.2. Trait 5: Style

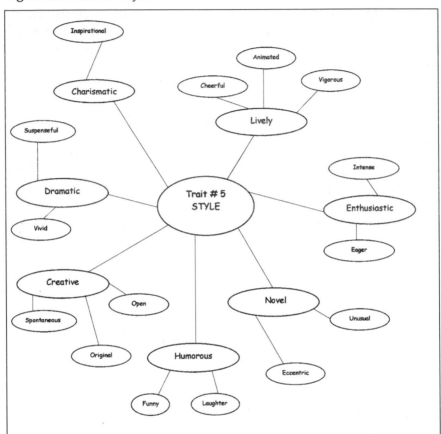

conservative pumps. My bulletin boards were masterpieces and my lesson plans were turned in on time. Mr. Truitt, in contrast, was what you might call a character. He had joined the ranks of teaching after working in construction, and when I became his grade-level partner he was already well into what I thought was advanced middle age. He smoked smelly cigars, read the *Chicago Sun-Times* (not the conservative *Chicago Tribune*), and told off-color jokes designed to embarrass me. His white shirts were never tucked in and his ties were frequently stained with egg yolk or gravy. His hair reminded me of a dirty mop and his hearty laughter frequently interrupted my carefully scripted lessons. I once heard him pounding on the chalkboard as he railed at his students, "Rabbits multiply faster than you people. Don't you know anything?" His class erupted in laughter. My students were jealous of all the fun they were having next door. Another thing that drove me crazy was the constant movement of his students' desks. Mr. Truitt was into groups of every kind and when he gave the signal, desks began careening around the room like bumper cars at Funway. He didn't take the curriculum guides and regulations as seriously as I did and he would frequently pop into my room after school to borrow something he had lost or to get help with a form that was due to the office. I felt like his secretary.

Mr. Truitt was memorable all right. Any student who ever had him for a teacher had a story to tell. He had a way with reluctant learners that was second to none. Squirrelly boys and girls with attitudes just couldn't escape his dogged persistence to get them to learn. He seemed to understand their natural distaste for anything that remotely resembled education and he camouflaged his lessons so they didn't look like lessons. He even had me fooled for a long time. His students were learning before they had time to remember that they hated school. He teased and cajoled them, gave them funny nicknames, wore strange hats, brought animals both dead and alive to school, and played baseball with his class during warm-weather recesses. I desperately wanted to be like him and at the same time I couldn't stand him.

Our love-hate relationship matured over the 5 years we worked together and I cried when I left Emerson School to take another job. He invited me back to make a speech at his retirement party and I cried again. If there was ever a teacher who personified teaching style, it was Mr. Truitt. He had flair, drama, personality, liveliness, charisma, creativity, and an especially keen sense of Irish wit. He wasn't always well groomed, liked a nip of scotch now and then (but never at school), and his cigar ashes were filthy, but I felt privileged to have worked next door to him for 5 years. In a way he set me free to find my own personal teaching style. I reasoned that if our principal tolerated his outrageous antics, I could certainly cut loose in the classroom once in a while. I began to play baseball at recess and allowed my natural sense of humor to emerge. I began to appreciate that teaching was about more than grading papers; it was about engaging students. I found my own unique style of teaching.

Almost 40 years after Mr. Truitt's intriguing style engaged students in the classroom next door to mine, style is still an important trait of the highly effective teacher. Every highly effective teacher has style, but each one must develop his or her own. Style cannot be cloned, copied, or even taught. The combinations and permutations of its various aspects are almost infinite. We will examine just three of the individual aspects of style in depth: humor, creativity, and novelty.

Humor

Of the personal dimensions of teaching, humor is the most human of all. Teachers who value humor, who not only tolerate laughter and fun in their classrooms, but even invite them in and encourage them to stay, are perceived by students as being more interesting and relevant than those who appear grim and humorless.

Kottler & Zehm (2000, p. 16)

The participants at one of my recent workshops, *How to Deal With Angry Parents,* were rolling in the aisles. The subject under discussion was an intensely serious one, but as the facilitator, I had decided to use a role-playing exercise to illustrate the heated emotions and stress that often accompany parent-educator interactions. One particularly dramatic principal-actress overdid her "angry parent" role just a bit, but the laughter served to relax the students, relieve some anxiety, and create bonds between me and the participants. A sense of humor is one of the qualities that is often mentioned by students when they are asked to list the qualities of their teachers that are most meaningful to them (Johnson, 1976).

Creativity

Teachers have to pick up where Sesame Street leaves off—without the colors, choreography, and guest appearances.

Linda Taylor

Creativity is about creating something new; about developing lessons that are unique; generating similes that sizzle; and making the mundane memorable. Creative teachers model the spontaneity of thinking and openness to new ideas that they desire in their students. I remember when Kathy Greider, then a fifth-grade teacher at Lincoln School and now a high school principal in central Illinois, decided to get creative with a yearlong interdisciplinary unit on garbage. When she first told me of her plan to apply for a grant that would give her funds to organize her instructional year around the themes of recycling, reducing, reusing, and so forth, I was a bit dubious. I questioned her judgment even more the day her class dug through mounds of Styrofoam trays and cold spaghetti to count and weigh the kinds and amounts of trash our students generated during lunch. Kathy was a creative teacher, no doubt about it. Her students reaped the academic benefits and their efforts even resulted in a new districtwide policy on recycling. The custodian thought the year would never end.

Novelty

All of the traits [of style] are important, but not necessarily in the same person. I have seen some excellent teachers who did not have flair and drama or liveliness. As Madeline Hunter said, "You don't need an elephant to teach the color gray."

Pam Conway

Novel teachers can seem idiosyncratic, eccentric, and even a little far-out. However, novelty doesn't have to be strange. Mr. Schuessler, a fourth-grade teacher at Lincoln School, rode his racing bike to school every day (a 10-mile one-way trip), and then, like Superman, changed into a mild-mannered teacher before the bell rang. Well, mild mannered, perhaps, but also novel. He used his mechanical talents to teach students how to repair and refurbish old bicycles during recess, lunch hours, and after school. Mrs. McCloughan, the other fourth-grade teacher, played college basketball. Her students loved to go one-on-one with her during teacher-taught gym periods. Her free-throw shooting expertise made her the talk of the playground.

"Sparkles" Reimann's style is hard to miss. Her one-of-a-kind outfits and spectacular jewelry dazzle first-graders, to say nothing of their parents. She concedes there probably isn't another teacher like her anywhere. Teacher of the Year in Missouri for 1997-98 and a 33-year veteran of the classroom, Carol Sue wears sparkling clothes and accessorizes with glittering jewelry to match. Even the most reluctant learners come to school with eagerness, wondering which dazzling outfit Mrs. Reimann will be wearing that day. Will it be the sequined fruit shirt for a lesson on food groups? Or will she don her flashy Fourth of July ensemble for a lesson on the symbols of America? Few teachers could (or would even choose to) pull off Sparkles's routine, but that's the wonder of highly effective teachers—they come in both subtle and sparkly packages.

Humor, creativity, and novelty aren't the only attributes of style. Here are some other ways that highly effective teachers demonstrate their style:

- The dramatic teacher is able to create suspense and make the mundane vivid and exciting.

- The enthusiastic teacher combines the qualities of intensity, eagerness, and fervor for the subject being taught.

- The lively teacher is animated, cheerful, and vigorous.

- The charismatic teacher possesses "a special quality of leadership that captures the popular imagination and inspires unswerving allegiance and devotion" (McKechnie, 1983, p. 305).

Substance or Style?

One often hears *substance* and *style* posited at opposite ends of a continuum, as though an individual with style must be a little light on substance. Some think that substance is solid and style is frivolous. I disagree. Since when is boring better? Style makes teachers stand out to their students as unique human beings. Style gives teachers a way to "hook" students, who, although they might find a certain subject boring or an assignment irrelevant, will nevertheless get involved because of who is teaching. Review Figure 3.2, found earlier in the chapter, to review the seven characteristics of style.

Recapping Chapter 3

Chapter 3 has described two of the four teaching traits that get results: with-it-ness and style. Throughout the discussion and examples in this chapter we have discovered that the highly effective teacher is a unique individual who not only brings personality and style into the classroom, but also creates an organized and well-managed environment where students are engaged and learning. Substance and style are not mutually exclusive traits. Highly effective teachers have both. Remember that you can also find a complete set of graphic organizers for all of the traits in Resource A.

Looking Ahead

In Chapter 4 we examine the third of the four teaching traits: motivational expertise. It has been said that "you can lead a horse to water, but you can't make him drink." Some educators believe that you can make students come to school, but you can't make them learn. Highly effective teachers beg to differ. They are motivators par excellence.

4

Teaching Traits That Get Results

Motivational Expertise

Classrooms are dynamic and complex societies that are rife with expectations: expectations that teachers have for students, and that students have for teachers and for each other. These expectations explain a good deal of what we see when we visit a classroom—both the good and the bad, the productive and the wasteful. But the expectations themselves can't be seen. They hang in the air almost like an atmosphere; they exist only between people and comprise a part of their relationship.

Saphier and Gower (1997, p. 47)

This chapter is about expectations. The expectations factor is one reason why two schools with similar kinds of students in identical urban neighborhoods can have vastly different achievement test scores, school climates, and student behavior. At the Evergreen School, the principal and teachers believe that what they are doing is important. They know that their students must have the academic skills they are teaching to be successful in life, and they frequently explain to students how what they are learning will help them in the future. Staff members at Evergreen know they have the skills, both instructional and interpersonal, to help their students be successful. Teachers feel empowered to make a difference. They don't ever give up; their students soak up the energy, motivation, and positive attention that comes from knowing that their teachers care and simply will not permit them to fall through the cracks.

At Stonewall School, by contrast, the principal and teachers don't believe in much of anything. Sometimes they think their students would be better off just to get on with their lives if they hate school so much. They feel powerless to make a difference and communicate this constantly to students. In fact, the teachers feel like the failures they think their students are. They give up easily and are bitter about their dashed hopes and dreams. Their low expectations hang in the hallways of Stonewall School like noxious fumes.

Trait 6: Motivational Expertise

The highly effective teacher is a motivator par excellence who believes in his or her own ability to make a difference in the lives of students and relentlessly presses and pursues students to maintain the highest possible behavioral and academic standards.

> *When you're traveling, you know your destination, but periodically you check the map to make sure you're on course. If the driver is the only one who knows the destination, the passengers can get nervous. They get restless and start whining. "How much further? Are we there yet?" If the driver tells the passengers the route, the timeline, and the destination, they will travel with more enthusiasm and cooperation. It's the same in the classroom. Keep the goals visible, set the speed for attaining them, adjust for road bumps and obstacles, but inform the students about how and when you expect to arrive at the destination.*
>
> Marsha Arest

I have chosen to frame our discussion of expectations as a motivational issue. Unless students (no matter what their ability level) feel the power, press, and urgency of their teachers' expectations, they are unlikely to be motivated to do even the minimum that is needed to make it in school, much less excel to the highest levels. Highly effective teachers motivate students in three ways:

1. Through their personal teaching efficacy

2. Through high behavioral expectations for students

3. Through high academic expectations for students

Figure 4.1 displays Trait 6, Motivational Expertise.

Personal Teaching Efficacy

For teachers to feel instrumental in their students learning, they must be certain of their practices, and they must hold a high sense of personal teaching efficacy; that is, they must believe that they have the capacity to directly affect a student's performance.

Kameenui & Darch (1995, p. 14)

It is one thing to develop a mission statement that includes the phrase "all students can learn"; it is quite another to translate those simple words into consistent teacher actions that actually convince students to believe and act on them. This strong personal belief in one's ability to make a difference in the lives of students is called efficacy. Webster defines efficacy as "the power to produce effects or intended results" (McKechnie, 1983, p. 578). The research shows that there is a strong relationship between teachers' efficacy and their students' achievement (Armor et al., 1976; Ashton & Webb, 1986; Berman, McLaughlin, Bass, Pauly, & Zellman, 1977).

For teachers to motivate students—particularly those students who lack intrinsic motivation, see little reason to achieve in school, or those students who have experienced high levels of frustration and failure—they need three qualities:

1. A strong and very specific set of beliefs or values with regard to learning and teaching

2. Research-based instructional methodologies and techniques

3. The energy and will to translate their beliefs and knowledge into actions

Figure 4.1. Trait 6: Motivational Expertise

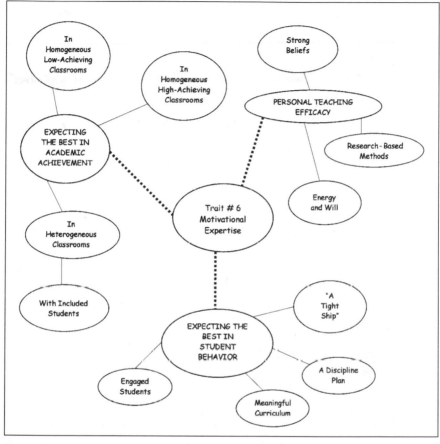

Beliefs About Learning and Teaching

Highly effective teachers get results when their less-effective colleagues do not because they teach with a totally different mindset. Kameenui and Darch (1995) identified six beliefs about teaching and learning that teachers with efficacy possess:

1. The learner must always be treated with respect.

2. Every learner has the capacity to learn.

3. The learner's behavior is purposeful, strategic, and intelligent.

4. The teacher makes a difference in how, what, when, and why students learn.

5. Good teaching involves creating as many opportunities as possible for successful learning.

6. Effective teaching enhances what the learner already knows and enables the learner to do things that could not be done before. (pp. 13-17)

Reliance on Research-Based Methods

Most teachers want to be effective teachers. They go to workshops, talk with colleagues, and try to find better ways to teach. However, the information that many of these teachers get is not good. Part of the problem is that they have not been taught how to judge good teaching— the basic principles. So, when they go to hear a particular speaker they can't evaluate the technique being presented. If it sounds exciting, if the students will like it, and if it is feasible they try it in their classrooms with good intentions. Knowledge of the basic principles of learning that have been proven with research is needed first.

Jeanne Wanzek

Teachers are unable to either develop a sense of efficacy or reinforce the feelings of efficacy they do have unless they can see the results of their teaching evidenced in the achievements of students. This is a major stumbling block for many new teachers. They graduate from college believing that all students are capable of learning, but suddenly discover that they don't have the instructional tools to translate that belief into reality. To reconcile their growing loss of efficacy, they begin to blame the problems they face on the learner's ability, learning style, motivation, or learning history. This philosophical shift doesn't happen dramatically. The slide into low efficacy may take several years, but gradually the teacher feels less and less able to make a difference. "To assume that a problem is inherent in the learner leaves the teacher without any influence, because the problem is framed as being outside of the teacher's province of control" (Kameenui & Simmons, 1990, p. 13). Highly effective teachers assume that if the skills, concepts, information, or ideas they have taught are not acquired, mastered, or retained, then there must have been something amiss with the instructional delivery system. They keep looking for answers until they find them. They do not blame the student's lack of ability or motivation.

Energy and Will

Our team held high expectations for our students—too high, many people said. Don't ask for too much, they warned. Passing grades and graduation would be good enough. But we wanted more. We asked our students to come to school every single day, to stay away from drugs and alcohol, to change their bad habits, to complete every classroom and homework assignment, to resist the pressure to join gangs, to give up their bad attitudes and clean up their language. We asked for everything we could think of, and they gave us everything they had.

Johnson (1995, pp. ix-x)

In addition to strong beliefs in their abilities to make a difference and their reliance on teaching methods that get results, highly effective teachers have an abundance of physical and mental energy as well as strong wills. This "instructional tenacity" (Kameenui & Darch, 1995, p. 13), relentlessness, or academic press[1] is nothing more than dogged persistence. Haberman (1998) believes that "star" teachers, as he calls them, "persist in trying to meet the individual needs of the problem student, the talented, the handicapped and the frequently neglected 'gray area' student. Their persistence is reflected in an endless search for what works best with each student" (p. 4). This quest for success for every student can be seen in a variety of very specific teacher behaviors:

- Establishing warm and encouraging relationships with students

- Treating students fairly, firmly, and with consistency

- Relying on their personal authority rather than constantly sending students to the dean or principal for discipline

- Using direct, non-emotional management techniques

- Never trying to embarrass students

- Treating all students as capable and trustworthy

- Maintaining a consistent emphasis on instruction and the importance of learning

- Maintaining a consistent effort to keep students on-task, interested, and aware of their individual accomplishments

- Teaching all of the students in the class, pushing them and monitoring their work

- Maintaining a constant sense of determination not to accept the failure of students (Ashton & Webb, 1986, pp. 84-86)

Expecting the Best in Student Behavior

> *When I walk into the classroom, I assume good behavior; I am rarely disappointed.*
>
> Adrienne Hamparian Johnson

The second way in which a skilled teacher expresses high expectations has to do with the teacher's attitudes regarding student behavior. You may have wondered, as you glanced through the table of contents before you began to read this book, why *discipline* didn't appear in any of the ten traits. "How can someone be a highly effective teacher without a discipline plan?" you asked. Believe me, I am all for articulating behavioral expectations to students and parents and letting them know what the consequences of violating the rules will be. Discipline plans were required of the teachers at Lincoln School. However, the highly effective teachers rarely had to rely on a printed set of rules to get the best out of their students, and the ineffective teachers had no idea how to even put their paper plan into action. Behavior plans are like insurance policies—you need them as a fallback in case some terrible emergency arises. For the skilled teacher, however, good behavior is the natural consequence of (a) engaged students; (b) meaningful curriculum; (c) a well-organized and managed classroom—that is, "a tight ship"; and (d) clearly stated expectations (a discipline plan). If the teacher has assessed what students already know and is then enabling them to do and know things they couldn't do and didn't know before they arrived in the classroom, there won't be time for misbehavior. Everyone will be too busy experiencing success. Furthermore, a desire to act responsibly will flow from the expectations of the teacher.

You may be raising your eyebrows at my naïveté, but consider Linda Taylor and Robert. You were introduced to them earlier. Robert had experienced dozens of discipline and behavior plans written by the myriad of psychologists, behavior-management specialists, and special-education teachers who tried to "fix" him. None of them were successful in changing his behavior. Sometimes he was so violent, two or three adults were required to restrain him. Only when he began to experience academic success did his behavior change. Linda never had a single behavior problem with Robert at all in four years. In fact, he won a citizenship award from the principal.

The highly effective teacher is a behavior motivator and instructional manager rather than a disciplinarian. The highly effective teacher believes that every learner's behavior is purposeful, strategic, and intelligent. You might not see Robert's violent outbursts as purposeful and intelligent, but they served his purposes rather nicely. He was finally moved to a setting where he learned to read. If Robert had been acquiescent and cooperative, he would still be illiterate!

Expecting the Best in Academic Achievement

> *No matter what you teach or how you present yourself to students, you have to be on the learner's side and to believe that they can and will grow during the time you are together.*
>
> Kohl (1984, p. 5)

Expectations are inferences that teachers make about students' future academic achievement and about the types of classroom assignments students need in relation to teachers' perception of their abilities. Expecting the best in academic achievement is the third and final aspect of Trait 6: Motivator par Excellence. Teacher expectations may concern either the entire class, groups of students, or individual students. What does the teacher with low expectations do differently than a teacher with high expectations? That may well depend on where the teacher is working. There are three kinds of classrooms in which most teachers find themselves, each with its own unique low expectations trap.

Expectations in Homogeneous
High-Achieving Classrooms

In a homogeneous class of high-achieving students such as one might typically find in an affluent suburban, highly selective private, or urban magnet school, teachers can make the mistake of thinking they don't have to worry about expectations. After all, their students have been programmed since preschool to plan for college, and they arrive in kindergarten prewired with their personal set of high expectations. Oh, there are a few challenging students here and there, but a critical mass of highly motivated students provides a momentum and impetus to academic achievement that can lull any teacher into a false sense of security. Teachers who work with generally high-achieving students look effective no matter what they do. Or, they may think they do.

In the state of Tennessee where achievement tests in every subject are given every year in every grade, some school districts evaluate not only actual test scores, but also consider what is called a value-added score (Sanders & Rivers, 1996). This second score quantifies how much learning value a specific grade level of school has added to what the students had when they arrived in the grade. For example, the comparison of two schools with identical demographics might reveal that both had overall high test scores, but received very different value-added scores. This alerts educators to the first kind of low-expectations trap: teachers who have put a ceiling on how much "smart" kids can learn. There are lots of very bright students coming to school and not learning much of anything they didn't know before they arrived because their teachers have failed to push them.

Expectations in Homogeneous
Low-Achieving Classrooms

In the second type of classroom, a homogeneous class of low-achieving students, such as one might typically find in urban schools or suburban and rural schools with urban demographics, teachers can fall into a low-expectations trap of an entirely different nature. Teachers whose classrooms are crowded with students who are skill deficient, have unproductive school behaviors, lack organization, and have low motivation need more than just a fancy slogan or good intentions to engage their student in learning. Over the years, lowered expectations for many low-income students and students of color have resulted in a sense of educational powerlessness and meaninglessness for huge numbers of students (Fine, 1991). The greater the number of low performers in a classroom, the less certain teachers felt about their ability to influence learning and achievement (Smylie, 1989). These teachers, demoralized by their lack of effectiveness, turn to unspoken agreements with students (e.g., I won't bother you if you don't bother me). The bromide of heightened expectations is increasingly ineffective in environments where low expectations are multigenerational and institutionalized (Ennis, 1998). Paulo Freire, the revolutionary Brazilian educator, describes how teacher-imposed expectations make disenfranchised learners feel.

> If teachers are consistently authoritarian, then they are always the initiators of talk, while the students are continually subjected to their discourse. They speak to, for, and about the learners. They talk from top to bottom, certain of their correctness and of the truth of what they say. And even when they talk with learners, it is as if they were doing them a favor, underlining the importance and power of their own voices. (Freire, 1998, p. 65)

Highly effective teachers understand that their power to raise expectations in challenging classroom settings comes as much from what they do and how they build relationships with students as from what they say. Stephen Covey (1990) suggests that "our personal integrity or self-mastery is the basis for our success with others" (p. 77).

High expectations are about far more than assemblies, raps, and cheers. They are about highly skilled teachers constructing classroom cultures in which students, who do not come to school with built-in expectations and confidence, can succeed. Here are some ways in which master teachers raise expectations in challenging classrooms:

1. Understand the students' backgrounds and the constraints and opportunities they provide for learning.

2. Provide numerous opportunities for legitimate academic success early in the school semester or year. Focus initially on students' strengths and use those strengths to build student confidence and scaffold later learning tasks.

3. Explain the grading system with concrete examples that demonstrate to students how they might enhance their grade. Confront the issue of low or failing grades by explaining the situation

that led to the grade and providing an alternative or second chance for students to complete the work, thus learning important study, writing, or test-taking skills useful in future assignments.

4. Construct sequenced learning tasks that facilitate skills acquisition in the subject area and remediate skills both within and outside of the subject when necessary to promote student success.

5. Make sure that every lesson includes positive, affirming ways of interacting with students and insist that they treat each other with the same level of courtesy.

6. Provide frequent opportunities for students to express their goals and aspirations for learning. Assist students to set positive, realistic goals and envision a successful future. Use these clues to build shared expectations to which both teacher and students can aspire. (Ennis, 1998, p. 177)

Expectations in Heterogeneous Classrooms

Many teachers have a sense of accountability to teach most of their students. If a large number of the students in the class do not learn a skill, most teachers blame themselves and try a different way to teach it. However, when there are just a few students who don't understand a lesson, many teachers don't blame themselves (because the other students learned it) and instead think there is something wrong with the student (e.g., they must need special services). Effective teachers realize that all students can learn if given the right instruction.

Jeanne Wanzek

The third kind of classroom can be found anywhere (e.g., urban, rural, or suburban schools) and contains a mix of students of every ability level. Teachers in these settings have to guard against differential expectations: having one set of expectations for their high-achieving students and a totally different set for low-achieving students. Brophy and Good (1974) document the following behaviors that communicate an "I don't expect much from you" attitude to students:

■ Waiting less time for low achievers to answer questions

■ Responding to low achievers' incorrect answers by giving them the answer or calling on someone else to answer the question more frequently than high achievers

■ Criticizing low achievers more frequently than high achievers

■ Praising low achievers less frequently than high achievers

■ Not giving feedback to public responses of low achievers

■ Paying less attention to low achievers

■ Calling on low achievers less often

■ Seating low achievers further from the teacher

■ Demanding (expecting) less from low achievers (pp. 330-333)

Expectations for Included Students

A final issue to be considered in the discussion of teacher expectations relates to the inclusion of special-education students in the regular classroom. What kind of expectations should teachers have for included students? Although there are few educators who would argue with the notion that inclusion provides enhanced opportunities for socialization and increased self-esteem for students with disabilities, as well as the security and stability of attending their home school, there are many who question whether this approach maintains high expectations for achievement.

In some classrooms, education for students with disabilities, particularly those with learning disabilities, resembles the way business is conducted with low-achieving students in urban schools (e.g., I pretend I'm really teaching you what you need to know to be successful in the real world and you pretend that you're really learning it). Mercier, Jordan, and Miller (1994), for example, have shown that students with learning disabilities are likely to reach an academic plateau after 7th grade and usually achieve only one more year of academic growth in math performance from the 7th to the 12th grades.

Meichenbaum and Biemiller (1998) point out that although "differentiated instruction is needed to reverse this pattern . . . the current increased emphasis on mixing ability groups ('destreaming'), which results in less instruction being geared to student achievement levels, is unlikely to reverse this pattern" (pp. 48-49). There are no easy answers to these difficult questions, but highly effective teachers struggle daily to find them. Less effective teachers don't care.

Highly effective teachers do not merely set forth their expectations and let those students who are unmotivated or less able fail. Nor do they have one set of expectations for high-achieving students and another for low-achieving students. Highly effective teachers articulate their expectations and then provide supportive, systematic instruction that enables every child to achieve far more than that child would have with low expectations.

What Did You Expect?

Some teachers pose this question when they overhear gossip in the teachers' lounge about a former student who has failed another course or been suspended one more time. "What did you expect?" they say, throwing up their hands. "I could have told you so."

Here's what I always answer to the question: "What did you expect?"

"Well, actually I expected a whole lot more. I expected the student would be able to make the grade and stay in school. I expected that working as a team this staff could make a difference in this student's life."

Success for students, whether low-achieving or honor roll, is about expectations. Students who don't arrive at school with a built-in set of expectations need highly effective teachers to give them theirs.

Recapping Chapter 4

We have just explored one of the most critical, in my opinion, of the 10 traits: the ability of highly effective teachers to get results from students, who for any number of reasons would not be likely to achieve in other classroom settings. How do these teachers do it? First, by believing in their own ability to make a difference and then by setting high expectations for students that come built-in with a teacher who won't let them fail. Turn back to Figure 4.1, found earlier in the chapter, to review this important trait.

Looking Ahead

In Chapter 5, we consider the final trait in the Teaching Traits category: instructional effectiveness. This trait gets at the very essence of education—what teachers do when they teach. You will find all of the strategies, learning principles, and essential skills that instructionally effective teachers need. Can we nail down good teaching, put it under a microscope, or even begin to describe it? That is our goal in Chapter 5.

Note

1. Academic press refers to the extent to which school members, including students and teachers, experience a strong emphasis on academic success and conformity to specific standards of achievement (Lee, Smith, Perry, & Smylie, 1999).

5

Teaching Traits That Get Results

Instructional Effectiveness

No amount of good feeling is adequate without that pedagogical dimension, without students actually knowing more and being able to do more at the end of a school year than they could at the beginning.

Kohl (1998, p. 27)

The debate regarding how to determine if students are actually learning anything in schools is often heated and sometimes even acrimonious. A single test, say the critics, is too narrow, confined, and skill specific; it cannot take the measure of a student's learning. There is more to an education than what can be demonstrated by filling in a few bubbles with a number 2 pencil. Those with accountability on the brain are just as firm in their stance. How will we know that students are learning anything at all if we do not assess them? Both camps can make their points ad nauseum, but in the end, it is the teacher who should be most concerned about how much progress each student has made. "Can my students do things they couldn't do last year, last week, or even yesterday?"

"Is my teaching effective?" These are the questions that highly effective teachers ask themselves daily. Whatever measures are used—whether multiple and performance based, or multiple choice and standardized— proof of teaching effectiveness is in the students' knowing and doing. Instructional effectiveness is the key.

Trait 7: Instructional Effectiveness

The highly effective teacher is an instructional virtuoso: a skilled communicator with a repertoire of essential abilities, behaviors, models, and principles that lead all students to learning.

> *There are those who argue that the successful teacher ought to be more concerned with the affective side of students rather than with the growth of cognitive skills. To a degree, this attitude may be correct, but to a larger degree, it is not. Bedside manner is often touted as being very important to a doctor's success. But how many patients choose the doctor with a more pleasant bedside manner over a doctor with a higher patient survival rate?*
>
> Scheidecker & Freeman (1999, p. 35)

Highly effective teachers don't teach in just one way—they have a repertoire of instructional techniques, teaching behaviors, and essential skills on which to draw, depending on the needs of their students, the nature of the subject, and the complexity of the learning outcomes. The knowledge and research that presently exists to inform the practice of teaching is rich. We do not know nearly all that we need to know, by any means. However, we do know a great deal about what works. To perfect and polish a teaching repertoire takes time, experience, practice, quality staff development, and highly skilled clinical supervision from peers and administrators. The sheer magnitude of what a teacher must know and do to be considered effective is mind-boggling. That is why I have chosen *virtuoso* to describe the instructionally effective teacher.[1] A virtuoso, according to Webster, is "a person having great technical skill in some fine art, especially in the performance of music" (McKechnie, 1983, p. 2042). The virtuoso teacher designs and executes a great lesson much like a virtuoso violinist performs a concerto.

The truly effective teacher knows how to execute individual behaviors with a larger purpose in mind. The larger purpose requires placing behaviors side by side in ways that accumulate to create an effect greater than can be achieved by a single behavior or small set of them. This is why teaching involves a sense of timing, sequencing, and pacing that cannot be conveyed by any list of behaviors. (Borich, 2000, p. 31)

As limiting as lists may be, there still remains the necessity for articulating those skills, abilities, behaviors, teaching approaches, and principles that, when skillfully employed, hold a strong likelihood for gaining the results that all teachers want to see. The virtuoso violinist has a vast repertoire of compositions, practiced and polished to perfection—from which the violinist can select to present a concert. The virtuoso teacher also needs a repertoire—a selection of teaching techniques. There are five components to the highly effective teacher's repertoire:

1. Communication abilities

2. Seven essential teaching skills

3. Multiple research-based teaching behaviors

4. A variety of well-executed teaching models or approaches

5. Twenty-four principles of learning

Figure 5.1 gives you a graphic preview of the "big picture" of instructional effectiveness. In addition to Figure 5.1, you will find six other graphic organizers in this chapter—evidence of the extent and complexity of Trait 7.

Communication Abilities

Identify a pool of highly successful teachers and you will be surprised to discover how very different they are as persons and as professionals. . . . As different as these highly successful teachers may be, there is one critical feature they share: they are all accomplished communicators.
                                                                    Kottler & Zehm (2000, p. 65)

I experienced a great deal of ambivalence when I first thought about the ability to communicate as it relates to highly effective teachers. At the

Figure 5.1. Trait 7: Instructional Effectiveness

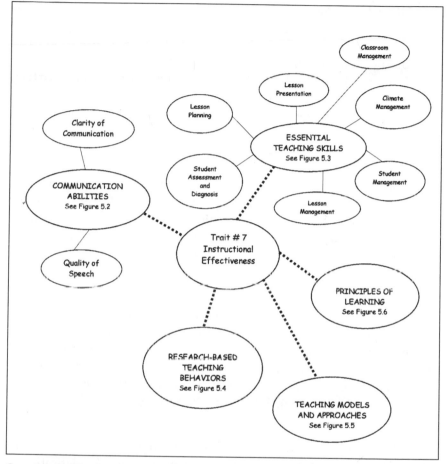

outset, I concluded that communication should be a trait unto itself, and that all of the interpersonal skills would then be subsumed under it. I reasoned that communication is far more than just "telling and talking"; it includes listening, understanding, caring, and developing relationships with students, colleagues, and parents. It is teaching with your mouth shut (Finkel, 2000).

After some additional reading and reflection, however, I decided that these interpersonal skills should more appropriately be grouped together under the real and positive person trait. Having made that decision, I then determined that some aspects of communication are a part of the mental life of effective teachers. I use *mental life* in the sense that teachers must be able to think about the act of teaching, as well as to be able to articulate what they are thinking to others. When you read the next chapter, you will find that the quality of being communicative (i.e., able to talk about what you are thinking or doing) is included there.

I was still left, however, with an aspect of communication that was different from communicating on an interpersonal level and also different from communicating on a metacognitive level. This third aspect of communication has to do with the ability to present to students in the classroom—the communication that goes on in the name of instruction.

Steve Linhardt has been teaching history and political science for seven years at the suburban Chicago high school from which he graduated. When asked about the importance of communication in his teaching, he touched on all three of the aspects I just mentioned.

> When I was in high school most of the teachers lectured all period. There was relatively little student interaction, so a teacher's ability to communicate the lesson to his/her students was vital. Today, I try to engage my students with role playing, simulations, and discussions, along with the lectures. Yet, without being able to effectively communicate to my students, I don't think they would get a whole lot out of the experience.

As Steve discussed the relationship between his ability to communicate and his effectiveness as a teacher, he seemed to imply a definition of communication that is limited to "teacher talk." In practice, however, he indicated his understanding that teachers are communicating even when they don't look like they are teaching (e.g., my teacher colleague, Mr. Truitt). The skills needed to orchestrate a successful role-playing experience or to facilitate a meaningful simulation are in reality far more demanding and sophisticated than simply standing in front of students and talking.

Steve also knows, however, that communication is not just one-way, nor is it solely confined to the topics in American history that he teaches. Inherent in any definition of communication is the idea that listeners have received, understood, and acted on what has been communicated. Steve explains with the following:

My communication skills help me to develop trust within my class. I know that students hate classes where they are confused. By effectively communicating, I think students feel more comfortable with me because they understand what is going on and what my expectations are. Also, being able to listen to my students makes me more effective because they can see that I care about them. This helps to create rapport and a sense of trust.

While Steve reflected on the importance of continuing to improve his communication abilities as he gains teaching experience, he was actually engaging in the more metacognitive aspects of communication—talking to oneself.

Many times, after a lesson does not go as well as I would have liked, I sit down and figure out a better way to explain something, or better questions to ask. This type of processing greatly enhances my effectiveness in communicating.

The communication abilities that teachers need to teach include "presenting new material, explaining concepts, giving directions or explaining directions when they need to be elaborated, activating prior knowledge, re-explaining old material, dealing with student confusions, and making connections during instruction" (Saphier & Gower, 1997, p. 189). Notice that all of the actions in this list carry with them the assumption that students will understand, know, or be able to do more as a result of what the teacher has done.

Highly effective teachers are models of instructional clarity. They use such explanatory devices as "analogies, highlighting important items, mental imagery, physical models, media/technology, use of charts or the blackboard, translation into fuller or more precise language, modeling thinking aloud, use of simple cues, use of progressive minimal cues, and graphic organizers" (Saphier & Gower, 1997, p. 198). When teachers are vague and confusing, their students do not learn as much (Smith & Land, 1981).

Agnes was the poster teacher for confused communication.[2] She never really committed herself to a position on anything. It was always "maybe, almost, could be, might be, pretty much, sort of, or possibly." She was constantly starting, stopping, regrouping, or retrenching. Just when I thought she might actually be heading off in the direction of a meaningful complete sentence, she would dangle the participle and leave her students hanging. When I reviewed the script of what she had said during a lesson, I felt as if I were in a "teaching twilight zone" or trying to nail down a piece of Jell-O. Agnes was a master of what Smith and Land (1981) call mazes—false starts or halts in speech, redundant words and tangles of words. Highly effective teachers, in contrast, make the complicated seem simple and the difficult downright easy. They are masters of foreshadowing, transitioning, and summarizing. They move smoothly through their presentations, rarely interrupting, distracting, or confusing themselves.

Another important aspect of the ability to communicate is the teacher's speech. Diction, pronunciation, enunciation, intonation, grammar, syntax, and choice of vocabulary are all critical contributors to effective communication. Highly effective teachers are excellent role models for their students. They do not talk above their students, but they often use challenging vocabulary in context and guide their students to new levels of spoken literacy. Figure 5.2 displays the variety of communication abilities in a graphic organizer. I have arbitrarily made some decisions in its construction that are open to interpretation or discussion. For example, I included foreshadowing, transitioning, and summarizing as part of making connections during instruction. A case could also be made for placing these strategies with either explaining concepts or giving directions.

Essential Teaching Skills

I love the look I see in kids' eyes when they comprehend something new or suddenly catch on to a concept that had previously confused them.
                                                                    Linda Taylor

The essential teaching skills are seven areas of expertise in which teachers absolutely must excel to be effective. These skills must be learned, practiced, improved, honed, and perfected. Individual teachers may vary somewhat in their abilities to execute these skills, but highly skilled teachers are able to fluently and automatically execute them seamlessly to create teaching performances that are flawless. Although some of these skills include aspects of instruction that we discussed in prior chapters, they bear repeating once more in this context.

Figure 5.2. Communication Abilities

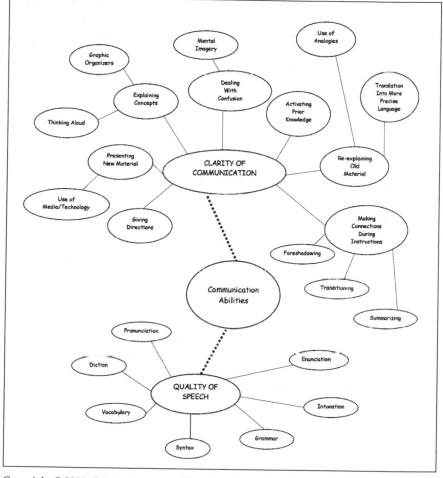

Lesson Planning

Highly effective teachers know how to plan and prepare lessons. They are able to articulate the objective(s) of the lesson, relate the current lesson to past and future lessons, and take into account the needs of their students and the nature of what they want to teach. Skillful teachers include components in their lessons that will attract their students' interest and keep them engaged. They are able to mentally walk through their lesson presentations beforehand, anticipating where problems of understanding or organization might occur and making adjustments up until the last minute.

Lesson Presentation

The ability to present lessons that have been planned is the second essential teaching skill. The excellent teacher utilizes good communication skills—giving clear explanation and instructions, asking questions that generate interest and stimulate thinking, and organizing an appropriate number and variety of learning experiences with which to engage students.

Lesson Management

Lesson management is the third essential teaching skill. This skill is different from presentation. Lesson presentation consists of all the things an observer (or student) can see and hear the teacher doing. Management, in contrast, is about the mental adjustments a teacher makes during instruction—the critical decisions with regard to fine-tuning the content, difficulty, or pace of the lesson. Lesson management is about making midcourse corrections in the flight plan to ensure that students do understand and do experience success.

Climate Management

The fourth essential teaching skill consists of creating a classroom climate or atmosphere that is positive, supportive, and focused on learning. This skill encompasses the communication of expectations, the encouragement of positive relationships, the motivation of students, and the development of team in the classroom—a skillful blending of the individual traits that we explored in Chapters 2 and 3.

Classroom Management

The next essential teaching skill is the ability to organize and manage the day-to-day operations of the classroom to maximize use of time and minimize off-task behavior. It includes the development of procedures and routines to keep the classroom running smoothly. Classroom management is the oil that lubricates instruction. With-it-ness is the trait that enables highly effective teachers to make it happen.

Student Management

The ability to deal swiftly and positively (in both proactive and reactive manners) with student behavior (or misbehavior) is essential teaching skill number six. The highly effective teacher is able to handle conflict and confrontation with authority, calm, and confidence. The highly effective teacher is also able to prevent, forestall, anticipate, and disarm disciplinary problems with students.

Assessment and Diagnosis

Assessing students' progress with a view to diagnosing and remediating or enriching, is the seventh and final essential teaching skill. Highly effective teachers are constantly evaluating their own teaching performance through assessing what their students have learned. This cyclical and ongoing process acts as a means of quality control for the teacher, enabling the teacher to fine-tune whole-class lessons, plan for additional small-group instruction, or make more major changes to curriculum, learning experiences, or instructional objectives. Review Figure 5.3, which summarizes the essential teaching skills.

Donna Garner, high school English and Spanish teacher in Texas, explains how she keeps constant tabs on her students' progress.

> We do lots of oral activities together so that students can't "hide." Every student must participate and is called on frequently. I believe in daily accountability particularly with my freshmen students who need short-term goals to keep them moving in the right direction. I monitor students' progress constantly so that I can spot concepts that need to be retaught or target students who need individual help before too much time has gone by.

Research-Based Teaching Behaviors

Teaching seems to be one of the last professions to emerge from the stage of "witch doctoring" to become a profession based on a science of human learning, a science that becomes the launching pad for the art of

Figure 5.3. Essential Teaching Skills

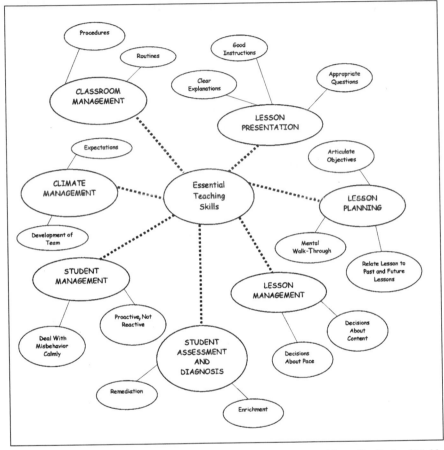

teaching. Only recently, however, has long-established research in learning been translated into cause-effect relationships of use to teachers. Only recently have teachers acquired the skills of systematically using these relationships to accelerate learning.

Hunter (1984, p. 169)

Although we know a great deal more today about effective instruction than we did 30 years ago, many educational researchers are still far more guarded in their statements regarding cause and effect than Madeline Hunter, the grande dame of staff development, was when she made the previous statement. Most researchers caution against writing specific prescriptions for teaching practices (Brophy & Good, 1986). There is, however, an extensive body of literature to recommend a number of research-based teaching behaviors. Figure 5.4 displays the teaching behaviors that, when skillfully integrated and executed by highly effective teachers, increase the likelihood that students will learn more efficiently. I have divided the behaviors into three categories:

1. Things the teacher must do

2. Things that the lesson must have

3. Things that the student must be

A lesson can be planned and sequenced and the teacher can have well-conceived goals in mind, but if the students aren't engaged and successful—the teacher cannot be considered highly effective.

Borich (2000) cites five behaviors that show promising relationships to desirable student performance, primarily as measured by classroom assessments and standardized tests:

1. Designing lessons that are clear and meaningful

2. Providing instructional variety

3. Being oriented to time on-task and task completion

4. Engaging students in the learning process

5. Ensuring a high rate of student success (Brophy, 1989; Brophy & Good, 1986; Dunkin & Biddle, 1974; Rosenshine, 1971; Teddlie & Stringfield, 1993; Wallberg, 1986)

Brophy and Good (1986), although cautionary in their approach to interpreting any direct cause-and-effect relationships between isolated teacher behaviors and student achievement, do conclude that "students learn more efficiently when their teachers first structure new information for them and help them relate it to what they already know, and then monitor their performance and provide corrective feedback during recitation, drill, practice, or application activities" (p. 368). The direct role of the teacher in designing lessons and providing clear and unambiguous

Figure 5.4. Research-Based Teaching Behaviors Related to Student Achievement

instruction needs to be reinforced and thoroughly appreciated. Highly effective teachers do not merely facilitate learning. They must also design, direct, and orchestrate it. "Effective teachers are clear about what they intend to accomplish through their instruction, and they keep these goals in mind both in designing the instruction and in communicating its purposes to the students" (Porter & Brophy, 1988, pp. 81-82).

Brophy and Good (1986) remind educators of the dangers of assuming that structured instruction is only appropriate for teaching low-level skills. Many teachers, trained to prefer indirect instructional methods, often fail to recognize that "even for higher level, complex learning objectives, guidance through planned sequences of experience is likely to be more effective than unsystematic trial and error" (Brophy & Good, 1986, p. 366). They further point out that systematic teaching does have an important role to play in the development of learning-to-learn skills, creative writing, and even artistic expression. They suggest that

> effective instructors working at higher levels must develop apt analogies or examples that will enable students to relate the new to the familiar or the abstract to the concrete; identify key concepts that help to organize complex bodies of information; model problem-solving processes that involve judgment and decision making under conditions of uncertainty; and diagnose and correct subtle misconceptions in students' thinking. (p. 366)

They explain that "these are complex, demanding, and yet essential activities, and should neither be demeaned as intrusive 'talk' nor confused with the relatively simple 'telling' or giving of 'right answers' that occur in basic skills lessons in the early grades" (Brophy & Good, 1986, p. 366).

Carol Jago has discovered the truth of Brophy and Good's statement. In *With Rigor for All: Teaching the Classics to Contemporary Students*, she says, "It began to dawn on me that if I wanted students to achieve deep literacy . . . , I was going to have to experiment with a dangerous practice, 'direct instruction.'" (Jago, 2000, p. 37). Carol goes on to explain.

> Maybe the reason non-honors students didn't have the "reading skills" teachers deemed necessary for negotiating the classics was that we hadn't taught them very well. I am not speaking here about teaching students how to read but rather about teaching students how stories work. In our urgency to abandon the lecture format, literature teachers may have adopted too passive a role. (p. 39)

Brophy and Good (1986) validate Carol's classroom experiences. They emphasize that

> there are no shortcuts to successful attainment of higher-level learning objectives. Such success will not be achieved with relative ease through discovery learning by the student. Instead, it

will require considerable instruction from the teacher, as well as thorough mastery of basic knowledge and skills which must be integrated and applied in the process of "higher level" performance. (p. 367)

Take time to review Figure 5.4, Research-Based Teaching Behaviors. The highly skilled teacher is able to execute these behaviors artfully—in a virtuoso teaching performance.

Ability to Select an Appropriate Approach

I see teachers grabbing left and right for the "brass ring," in hopes that they will find a formula, a list, or a solution for the problems of learning. They attend a two-hour presentation of some new idea, but, instead of going home to research it, and decide if it does have value, or even if only parts have value, they jump in with both feet, confusing their students more than ever.

Linda Taylor

There are more than 24 bona fide models of teaching and several methods or approaches to instruction from which highly skilled teachers can select to achieve their stated outcomes or objectives. One might doubt the truth of that statement, however, upon visiting randomly selected schools anywhere in the United States. In some settings, one sees only highly scripted lessons with intensive direct instruction. In other buildings, every lesson is taught in cooperative groups. In still another school, the teachers are standing behind their podiums lecturing from a sheaf of notes day after day, while across town, students are being taught solely to their preferred learning style. Highly effective teachers, quite rightly, use a variety of different methods. They are situational teachers, if you will. Ineffective teachers use just one approach, be it the one dictated by the principal, the "innovation du jour," or a method they have always used with little regard for effectiveness. When a single teaching methodology is exclusively mandated by administrators—whether totally traditional or completely constructivist (Brooks & Brooks, 1993)—highly effective teachers experience frustration, recognizing that one size never fits all. Skilled teachers are instructional eclectics, able to select the model or approach that best meets the demands of their content, their students, and their learning outcomes, and then execute it successfully with students. They are able to move back and forth with ease along a continuum of teaching models that ranges from teacher centered at one end to student centered at the other, but they are always subject centered no matter how they are teaching.

Saphier and Gower (1997) define a model of teaching as "a particular pattern of instruction that is recognizable and consistent . . . has particular values, goals, a rationale, and an orientation to how learning shall take place" (p. 271). They distinguish models that typically have the names of theorists affiliated with them (e.g., Carl Rogers's nondirective teaching or David Ausubel's advance organizers) from common patterns of instruction such as lecture or recitation.

Joyce and Weil (1996) have written the definitive book on teaching models and categorize the more than 24 models they describe into four distinct families:

1. Social

2. Information processing

3. Personal

4. Behavioral

They place models like cooperative learning and role-playing in the social family; models like strategic instruction or inquiry into the information-processing family; nondirective instruction in the personal family; and direct instruction along with mastery learning in the behavioral family.

Rosenshine and Stevens (1986) point out the necessity for varying the approach or model of teaching to match the content that is being taught and suggest criteria for decision making. When "the learning objective is to master a body of knowledge or learn a skill which can be taught in a step-by-step-manner (e.g., decoding skills, foreign-language vocabulary or grammar or musical notation)," structured and direct instruction is more effective. When the learning objective is more "ill-structured" such as "teaching composition, writing of term papers, analysis of literature, problem solving in specific content areas, discussion of social issues, or the development of creative responses" (p. 377), models that emphasize inductive and logical reasoning, group processing skills, or creative problem solving are more appropriate.

Figure 5.5 shows a variety of teaching models. The models shown are not meant to be exhaustive. For a comprehensive discussion of teaching models see Saphier and Gower (1997) or Joyce and Weil (1996).

Highly effective teachers differ from ineffective teachers in these important ways:

1. They use multiple models and approaches.

2. They continually add to and refine their repertoire of teaching models.

3. They choose an approach or model that best fits the content, the level of their students, and the objective they wish to achieve.

4. They develop their own unique models of teaching that specifically apply to their students and area of teaching.

5. They carefully consider new approaches that are introduced to them by evaluating research and examining results.

Ability to Apply the Principles of Learning

Modeling is the queen of instruction.

Pam Conway

Madeline Hunter was among the first to bring the principles of learning "to life" for classroom teachers. I had the privilege of being in her audience on many occasions. Highly effective teachers use many of these principles routinely, although the number of teachers who do not recognize Hunter's name today is often disheartening. Madeline did not invent the principles of learning, but she had the brilliance to collate the gems she gathered from great learning theorists of the past like Pavlov (1957), Thorndike (1913), Skinner (1953), and Watson (1925), and translate them into practical applications for teachers. Her works are still in print with titles like *Teach More—Faster* (1967c); *Motivation Theory for Teachers* (1967a); *Retention Theory for Teachers* (1967b); and *Teach for Transfer* (1971).

Here are just a few of the learning principles that Madeline illuminated for me:

Figure 5.5. Teaching Models

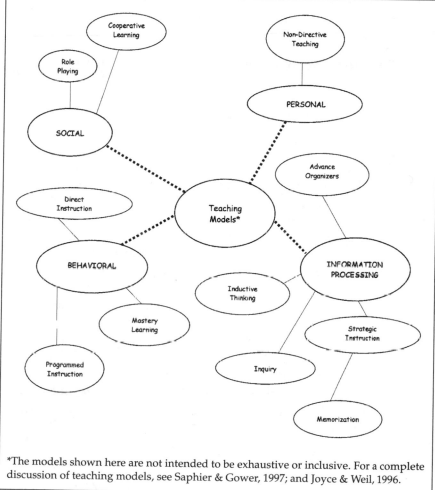

*The models shown here are not intended to be exhaustive or inclusive. For a complete discussion of teaching models, see Saphier & Gower, 1997; and Joyce & Weil, 1996.

■ "Meaning is one of the most important propellants of learning. Meaning, however, does not exist in material but in the relationship of that material to students' past knowledge and experience" (Hunter, 1982, p. 51).

■ "Knowing that amount of original learning is important to retention, we won't waste our students' time by going 'once over lightly,' but will see that important material is well learned" (Hunter, 1967c, p. 13).

■ "A learner's motivation increases as his success increases. You can make a student's success more probable by setting the task at the right level for him. Make sure that the assignment is not too difficult for some; they'll give up. The ones for whom the assignment is too easy will quit with boredom" (Hunter, 1976, p. 33).

Saphier and Gower (1997) have identified 24 learning principles, and each principle is packed with potential for learning power. I have displayed the principles graphically in Figure 5.6. You will recognize some of these "packages of power" (Saphier & Gower, 1997, p. 237), but others may be new to you. I highly recommend Saphier and Gower's discussion for any educator who wants to "teach more and teach it faster," as the title of Madeline Hunter's best-selling book proclaims (1967c). At no time have educators been under more pressure to increase student achievement. Achievement does not go up just because educators write more eloquent improvement goals, work longer and harder every day, or feel good about what they are doing. Achievement goes up when teachers teach more effectively and efficiently.

Highly effective teachers recognize that there are solid research-based learning principles that enable them to teach more and teach it faster; to teach so that students will retain what is taught; and to teach in ways that will gain the support and enthusiastic participation of all students in the learning process. Skilled teachers know and can talk about these principles, but more important, they apply them consistently in their classrooms.

Recapping Chapter 5

We have just explored a variety of tools that highly effective teachers use when providing instruction to students:

1. Communication abilities

2. Essential teaching skills

Figure 5.6. Principles of Learning

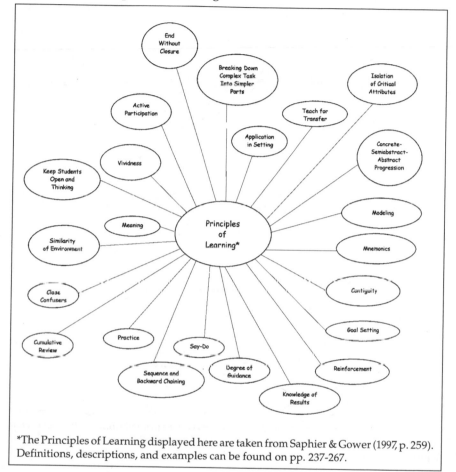

*The Principles of Learning displayed here are taken from Saphier & Gower (1997, p. 259). Definitions, descriptions, and examples can be found on pp. 237-267.

3. Research-based teaching behaviors

4. The ability to select and implement an appropriate teaching model or approach from a wide repertoire

5. The ability to apply specific principles of learning

Figure 5.7. Teaching Traits That Get Results

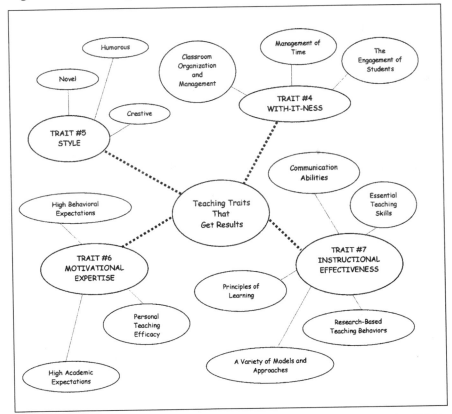

With the completion of this chapter, we have now examined all four of the teaching traits that get results: with-it-ness, style, a motivator par excellence, and instructional effectiveness. Figure 5.7 summarizes the complete package.

Looking Ahead

The highly effective teacher is more than just a person of character with highly developed teaching skills. The highly effective teacher is also brain based. Without teachers who have active mental lives, intellectual curiosity, and a solid knowledge base, classrooms will be intellectually impoverished. In Chapter 6, we explore the final group of traits: the intellectual traits that demonstrate knowledge, curiosity, and awareness.

Notes

1. The use of *virtuoso* to describe highly effective teachers is not original with me. Brophy & Good (1986) used this term in their review of the relationship between teacher behavior and student achievement.

2. Agnes is a composite of many teachers and is not intended to portray any single teacher with whom I have worked.

6

Intellectual Traits That Demonstrate Knowledge, Curiosity, and Awareness

The subject centered classroom is not one in which students are ignored. Such a classroom honors one of the most vital needs our students have: to be introduced to a world larger than their own experiences and egos, a world that expands their personal boundaries and enlarges their sense of community.

Palmer (1998, p. 120)

The intellectual abilities of teachers have long been fodder for humorists. "Those who can, do. Those who can't, teach," goes the familiar line. From time to time, there are articles in the news about the lack of academic rigor in education schools (e.g., inflated grade point averages and lower entrance requirements) or statistics regarding how many teachers failed to pass a state certification exam. In his classic Pulitzer Prize winning book, Richard Hofstadter charged that the teacher "has not only no claims to an intellectual life of his own, but not even an adequate workmanlike competence in the skills he is supposed to impart" (1963, p. 310). Over 30 years later, Craig and Aimee Howley (1995) find no reason to alter Hofstadter's assessment. In *Out of Our Minds: Anti-Intellectualism and Talent Development in American Schooling*, they include numerous studies detailing the intellectual deficiencies of teachers:

1. Graduate Record Examination (GRE) scores of prospective teachers rank lower that those of prospective nurses, biologists, chemists, aeronautical engineers, sociologists, political scientists, and public administrators (Schlechty & Vance, 1981; Vance & Schlechty, 1982; Weaver, 1978, 1979).

2. Prospective teachers take fewer upper-division courses in subjects other than pedagogy (Galambos, Cornett, & Spitler, 1985).

3. Teachers do not read very much (Duffey, 1973).

4. Teachers overwhelmingly prefer popular rather than scholarly or professional literature (Duffey, 1974).

In light of these distressing findings, perhaps we should not be surprised by the recurring question that teachers often hear: "If you're so smart . . . then why are you teaching?" (Owens, 1990).

Little Jimmy Delisle told his parents that he wanted to be a teacher when he was in first grade.

> They didn't say much. I said the same thing again in 2nd grade, and 4th grade, and especially in 8th grade (when Mr. Sheppard, my first guy teacher, was my hero). It was then at my 8th grade graduation party that Uncle Ray took me aside to offer some of the advice he was so prone to give. "Jim," he said, "you don't really want to be a teacher. There's no money in it. Besides, boys don't become teachers, girls do. . . . Jim, you're too smart to be a teacher." (Delisle, 1995)

There are lots of people who think that teaching is a job for people who aren't that smart.

Truth to tell, if teachers are going to be highly effective and not merely mediocre, they need to know a great deal. Shulman (1987) identifies seven different kinds of knowledge that highly effective teachers must have:

1. Knowledge about content

2. Knowledge about broad principles and strategies of classroom management and organization

3. Knowledge about curriculum materials and programs

4. Knowledge about the teaching of particular content topics

5. Knowledge about pupils

6. Knowledge about educational contexts, ranging from the classroom group to aspects of the community

7. Knowledge about educational aims and values (pp. 1-22)

Just ahead we examine the intellectual traits of highly effective teachers that demonstrate knowledge, curiosity, and awareness. I have dubbed these traits book learning, street smarts, and a mental life. Figure 6.1 provides a visual preview of the intellectual traits of highly effective teachers.

Trait 8: Book Learning

The highly effective teacher has a sound knowledge of content (the structure of the discipline) and outcomes (what the school, district, or state has determined is essential for students to know).

> *We should no longer be admitting students [into the profession] who have not excelled in a rigorous undergraduate education. Their transcripts should show convincing evidence that they worked hard to learn the discipline(s) they want to teach to those who have little idea what it includes.*
>
> Galluzzo (1999)

Student: If you're so smart, how come you're a teacher?

Teacher: To make sure you end up being smart too.

Student: Really?

Teacher: Sure. Kids who have smart teachers get higher test scores.

Student: No kidding?

Figure 6.1. Intellectual Traits That Demonstrate Knowledge, Curiosity, and Awareness

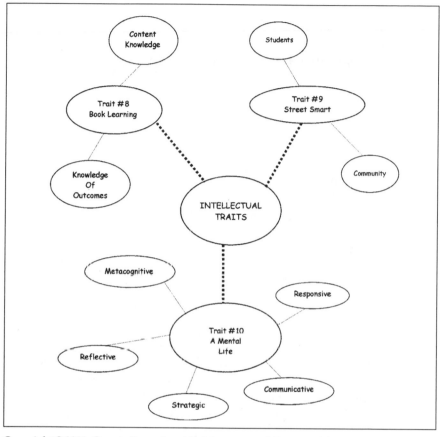

Teacher: In Texas, the literacy levels of teachers were more closely associated with student performance than any other inputs (Ferguson, 1998).

Student: But, we're not in Texas.

Teacher: Well, in Alabama the ACT scores of future teachers were the best predictors of the kinds of gains their students would make (Ferguson & Ladd, 1996).

Student: We don't live in Alabama either.

Teacher: Well, would you trust the Coleman Report?

Student: Maybe. If I knew what it was.

Teacher: It created quite a stir back in 1966 when it reported that teachers' scores on a test of verbal ability were the *only* school "input" to have a positive relationship to student achievement (Coleman, 1966; Jencks, 1972).

Student: Well, that's old stuff.

Teacher: How about if I told you that Linda Darling-Hammond, a Stanford University professor, found that the strongest predictor of how well a state's students performed on national assessments was the percentage of well-qualified teachers: educators who were fully certified and had majored in the subjects they taught (Darling-Hammond, 2000).

Student: Wow, *now* I know why *I'm* so smart. Because I've got a smart teacher.

Knowledge of Content

Deep knowledge includes knowledge about ways of representing and presenting content in order to foster student learning or construction of meaningful understanding.
                                    Einhardt, Putnam, Stein, & Baxter (1991, p. 88)

Highly effective teachers have content knowledge based on the accumulated literature and studies in their content area, as well as the historical and philosophical scholarship on the nature of knowledge in that content area (Shulman, 1987). This statement might seem applicable when talking about teachers of literature, mathematics, or physics. "However, what about first-grade teachers?" the skeptic may ask. Surely, these individuals need know nothing more than how to fill paste pots and cut construction paper. On the contrary, teaching 6-year-olds to read is far more complex and challenging than most laypeople realize. The highly effective first-grade teacher needs knowledge of phonetics, phonology, morphology, English orthography, semantics, and syntax (Moats, 2000). A solid knowledge of content is critical whatever the discipline or grade level.

Learning never stops for the highly effective teacher. Steve Linhardt, the high school social studies teacher we met earlier in the book, credits John Fuller, his high school history teacher, for motivating him to become a lifelong student of history. "Mr. Fuller told me that *his* personal goal was to read at least six historical volumes every school year," Steve reported. "I couldn't believe it." As a first-year teacher Steve barely had enough time to eat, let alone read books. In fact, he doubted he would ever have time to read again. However, as he has gained experience and confidence, he has also become an avid reader of books—books that add to his content knowledge.

Linda Taylor is a reader as well. She has an immense personal library of professional books and children's literature and reads several volumes every week. She is constantly seeking out methodologies and strategies that will unlock the learning, emotional, and behavioral problems of her students. When she finds an author she likes, she doesn't hesitate to contact that person to engage in further discussion. She soaks up knowledge like a sponge and is constantly marketing the joy of learning to her students. "Introducing my students to new knowledge is such fun. It is so exciting to model what learning looks like for them."

Kathleen Hoedeman believes strongly in the importance not only of content knowledge, but also of the role of the teacher in modeling how to learn for her students.

> Teachers are presumed to possess knowledge, but in order to teach effectively an educator must "know" deeply and well. But beyond the possession of knowledge there is something more— the joy of learning. A good educator will be seen among papers and books, scurrying toward the library, surfing the Internet, expressing delight over ideas, and struggling over solutions to tough problems. Most students need to see the joy of learning exemplified; once it is modeled, it becomes infectious. A student's well being depends on the teacher's possessed knowledge and willingness to continue learning—not only about the content area, but also about the student and about the field of education.

Knowledge of Outcomes

> *Mr. Turner has someone from the board giving us workshops, an educational chiropractor here to "align our curriculum." He had us*

write our "unit titles" on big pieces of newsprint, and then we hung them up in a row, so everyone could see how everyone's teaching fits in with everyone else's teaching. Basically, we were making lists of what our kids will know by the end of the year, by topic. I thought my list was pretty basic.

You can't possibly teach all you say you can teach. A teacher can teach a maximum of fourteen units per annum.

I pointed out to the board of ed guy, "Can't we write up our paperwork so it looks like we're following the state guidelines and do whatever we want?"

Codell (1999, pp. 137-138)

There are two major issues that confront every educator on a daily basis: what to teach and how to teach it. Increasingly, the question of what to teach is no longer in the hands of the teacher. State boards of education and legislatures are making the decisions. Many highly effective teachers are delighted with having a more definitive road map.

Adrienne Hamparian Johnson is one of them. She has not only digested every word of the Language Arts outcomes from the Illinois State Board of Education, she has developed brightly colored pages of "goals-at-a-glance" that she keeps within easy reach. "I want to be sure that I teach and assess everything my students are expected to know" (Johnson, reprinted by permission). For Adrienne, the outcomes have provided the opportunity to bring consistency and articulation to the language arts curriculum in her middle school. She has been working not only with her grade-level colleagues, but also with a district language arts committee, to ensure that their efforts are coordinated and articulated for Grades K-8.

Some highly effective teachers are less impressed with their state's outcomes. Donna Garner was deeply involved in the development and writing of the Texas Essential Knowledge and Skills (TEKS) for Language Arts at the state level. She and several committee members did their best to lobby for what they believed was a more rigorous and content-based set of outcomes. They subsequently wrote their own document that was well-received and reviewed by many (Garner, 1997). In the end, however, their document did not receive the needed votes from the State Board of Education to be adopted. When the outcomes became law, Donna resigned from the public high school where she had spent her entire career and is now teaching in a small private school. Outcomes, for Donna, are not just stacks of paper in three-ring binders. To her, outcomes are central to her efforts as a teacher. She has made a deliberate choice not to expend her energies holding students accountable for outcomes to which she is not personally committed. Donna could have chosen to do what many teachers do. "When the door is shut and nobody else is around, the classroom teacher can select and teach just about any curriculum he or she decides is appropriate" (English, 1992, p. 1). One must respect Donna's integrity, if not her courage. Highly effective teachers know the power of learning outcomes taken seriously.

Knowing Deeply and Well

What does it really mean for a teacher to know deeply and well? To Alan Jones, the principal of West Chicago High School (IL), it means that a teacher has thought about content; knows the essential and important concepts of the discipline that must be taught; and can make it come alive for students in ways that engage their minds.

> To me, this means presenting your discipline in such a way that a student who thought he knew what history was like and had already made up his mind that he didn't like it, suddenly becomes crazy about history because he's not hearing from the teacher what he expected to hear. He thought history was just a dull recitation of dates and this teacher is making it relevant and exciting.

Trait 9: Street Smarts

The highly effective teacher has knowledge of the students, the school, and the community in which the teacher is teaching and uses this knowledge to solve problems in the instructional setting: This teacher has street smarts.

> *Most teachers want to know more about their students. We want to understand what motivates them and makes them tick, what engages and interests them, and we want to know why they act as they do. We want to be more effective—to maximize those satisfying moments when we reach children, and minimize the frustrations of seeing everything we try fall flat. And while we have become accustomed to scores and*

grades, we often want to know more than we can possibly learn by relying on an objective impersonal standard, whether it be a grade-level average, a test result, or a letter or number assigned to potential or achievement.

Ayers (1993, p. 33)

I chose *street smarts* to describe this second aspect of knowledge that teachers need to be effective: knowledge about students, the school, and the community. My definition of street smarts for teachers also includes their knowing the rules, the language, and the culture of the students and parents with whom they work.

Street Smart Teachers

Lucia Leck teaches first grade in a small suburban community where visits to the homes of every student are routine for many teachers.[1] The visits usually take place before school begins in the fall, but must be completed before the first parent-teacher conference is held. The homes Lucia visits range in size from tiny apartments to five-acre estates, but she is not appraising property. She is getting to know her students so that she can be a more effective teacher. Lucia's quiet ways and gentle manner are disarming to both parents and students. She is relaxed and casual during her visits. However, her razor-sharp mind is filing away the kind of information and details about each child that would impress any ethnographic field-worker. As the school year unfolds, she will use all of this knowledge—to structure her teaching, respond to the unique needs of each child, and empathize with parents. Here is what Lucia does during her visits:

> Most of my time is spent with the child showing me his or her bedroom where I learn about the family, special interests, pets, and favorite books. Then we might go to the playroom or outside to see something special. Sometimes we will share a brownie or a special treat that the child has helped make. The visit always gives me a snapshot of what the child's life is like outside of school. I feel these home visits give me invaluable knowledge about my students.

Jerry Jesness, currently a special-education teacher for the Los Fresnos School District in the Rio Grande Valley (TX), believes that being a part of the community in which one teaches can provide insights impossible to achieve as a commuter.

> If possible, a teacher should live in a community of the type where his/her students live, not necessarily for life, but at least for a time. My first full-time teaching job was at Crazy Horse School on the Pine Ridge Reservation in Wanblee, SD. We nonnatives who lived on the reservation were teased by our students for being "bureau squatters," but we did get a perspective that teachers who commuted from off of the reservation did not.

Jerry also recommends becoming a student of the culture in which one is teaching. "Books offer windows to the lives of those that we teach. Teachers who teach students from cultural backgrounds that are different from their own would do well to study their history and literature."

Reading to Learn

Teachers should also consider reading in the discipline of anthropology.

> Among other things, the theoretical insights and techniques of anthropology offer educators sharpened awareness of the community context of the school, the significance of conflict between cultural ideals and realties, the problems of ethnic, race, and class relations as they affect education, and educational and cultural forces as they affect the developing child. (Fuchs, 1969, p. xi)

Here is a sampling of anthropological perspectives that offer important information about how students from different cultures may react and respond to typical "teacher talk" and teacher expectations.

- Lisa Delpit (1986, 1988, 1995) writes passionately about the need for teachers to help children not only appreciate communication patterns in their own cultures, but also to recognize the importance of their gaining proficiency in more formal and standard ways of speaking and writing.

■ Ruby Payne (1998) discusses the importance of understanding the hidden rules under which many of our students who live in poverty may be operating as well as the necessity for teaching them the rules that will help them be successful at school and work.

■ Shirley Brice Heath (1983) shares the insights she gained while living at length in two poor, rural communities in the South—one largely African American and the other White. She explains for her readers how students' ways of doing things in the classroom reflected the differences in their communities. She helps educators to understand these differences and to translate that understanding into more effective teaching.

These ethnographers have studied poor and working-class communities, but those who teach in upscale, affluent communities need their own version of "street smarts" as well. Teachers who work in communities where money is no object must understand and deal not with extreme poverty, but with wealth, power, and influence. They must regularly handle rigorously demanding and in-your-face parents who challenge the status quo. In suburban communities where CEO's and corporate attorneys abound, teachers must be able to explain what they are doing and why they are doing it logically and clearly. They must be able to accept constant questioning of their judgment and authority with equanimity and confidence. The cultural challenges in upscale communities are different from those experienced by teachers who work in urban areas; but they are no less demanding. Skilled teachers recognize that the more they know about their students and parents, the more likely they are to be successful in connecting with them in ways that will result in success for students—whether rich or poor.

Listen and Learn

Highly effective teachers are like good detectives. They are constantly searching for clues as to why students behave, communicate, and respond in the ways they do. They are gathering information that will help them to structure learning tasks, raise expectations, and gain the trust and respect of their students. In a sense, teachers must become students of their students—seeking to understand before they attempt to be understood (Covey, 1990).

Trait 10: A Mental Life

The highly effective teacher has a mental life that includes the abilities to be the following:

1. *Metacognitive:* able to read one's own mental state and then assess how that state will affect one's present and future performance

2. *Strategic:* able to think aloud and model strategic learning for students

3. *Reflective:* able to think about personal teaching behaviors for the purposes of self-growth

4. *Communicative:* able to articulate ideas, issues, beliefs, and values about the act of teaching with colleagues, students, and parents

5. *Responsive:* able to flex to the changing needs and demands of the profession

A teacher should have some interests beyond his or her specialty. In bearing, in manner of thinking and talking, a teacher should quite naturally appear to be a person with a mental life, a person who reads books and whose converse with colleagues is not purely business shop; that is, not invariably methods and troubles, but substance as well. There is no hope of attracting students to any art or science and keeping up their interest without this spontaneous mental radiation.

Barzun (1991, p. 98)

The final trait of the 10 traits of highly effective teachers, a substantive thought life or a mental life, is somewhat hard to pin down. One of the reasons for its elusiveness is that much of what constitutes the mental life of a highly effective teacher cannot be seen. Of course, observers can see the results—problems are solved, actions are taken, behaviors are evidenced. However, just exactly what went on in the teacher's mind to make all of those things happen so effortlessly is unknown. That is, unless the teacher is able to articulate it.

Metacognitive

Teaching is a complex cognitive skill. To be more precise, teaching is problem solving in a relatively ill-structured, dynamic environment.

Classroom teaching consists of a number of linked problem situations: the solution of one problem situation directly influences the next problem situation.

van der Sijde (1990, p. 63)

Metacognition is an aspect of teaching that cannot be seen. To be metacognitive is to be able to read one's own mental state and then to assess how that state will affect one's present and future performance. Being metacognitive is somewhat like having an inner coach. This inner voice "calls time-out at critical junctions . . . reviews game plans . . . selects and adapts specific strategies to meet changing task demands . . . monitors progress . . . and gives 'pep-talks' along the way" (Meichenbaum & Biemiller, 1998, p. 20). Metacognitive teachers, in a sense, have their own built-in teaching coaches. When they face a teaching dilemma or decision, their inner coach is there to pull them into a huddle and help them tinker with the problem, hypothesizing several ways to solve it, mentally walking them through several likely scenarios, and finally helping to firm up what to do when the time-out ends.

How can one tell if a teacher is metacognitive? Here are some ways in which metacognitive teachers differ from those who lack metacognitive skills.

- Metacognitive teachers are active, self-directed learners as well as active, self-directed teachers. Ineffective teachers are passive and inactive. Life just happens to the ineffective teacher. To be sure, metacognitive teachers are not easy. They question, think, discuss, create, and plan. They stir things up and are always pushing. Marsha Arest and Jaime Escalante are examples of metacognitive teachers. Their minds are always at work. They keep administrators on their toes.

- Metacognitive teachers are on-task and focused. Ineffective teachers are distractible, wasting time in their classrooms by constantly interrupting and disrupting their own teaching, yet unable to monitor and adjust their own behaviors.

- Metacognitive teachers have the big picture and get the big ideas of teaching and learning. Ineffective teachers just want recipes. They often respond to instructions or directions without fully understanding them. Ineffective teachers don't care whether students learn; they just want to cover the material.

■ Metacognitive teachers are independent and self-directed. Ineffective teachers are principal- or other-dependent. Consider how frequently ineffective teachers send students to the office for minor problems that should be handled in the classroom.

■ Metacognitive teachers hold conversations with mentors, principals, and colleagues that are idea and concept focused. Ineffective teachers need frequent task-directive speeches from their mentors, their coaches, and their principals and seem to lose the main idea shortly after the directions are given.

Meichenbaum and Biemiller (1998) have humorously suggested that less self-directed students seem to need "metacognitive prosthetic devices" or "surrogate frontal lobes," a transplant, if you will, to do their thinking for them because they are unable to plan, monitor, and guide themselves (p. 57). The same could be said of less-effective teachers. Highly effective teachers not only have strong metacognitive skills, but as we will discover in the next section, they are also able to teach these strategies to their students.

Strategic

Strategic behavior improves learning.

Strategic behavior can be taught.

Strategic behavior can be learned.

(T. Paris, personal communication, 1985)

Webster defines a strategy as "a skill in managing or planning" (McKechnie, 1983, p. 1799). A cognitive strategy is a skill in managing or planning one's learning. Cognitive strategies can be thought of as mental tools, tricks, or shortcuts to gaining meaning, understanding, or knowledge. They are also defined as "behaviors and thoughts that a learner engages in during learning that are intended to influence the learner's encoding process" (Weinstein & Mayer, 1986, p. 315). To be strategic as a learner means knowing how to choose and then access the appropriate cognitive strategy for the task at hand. To be a strategic teacher means not only being a strategic learner oneself, but also being able to think aloud, explain, model, and directly teach cognitive or learning strategies to one's students.

Although a good case could be made for including this aspect of highly effective teaching in one of the earlier chapters on teaching traits, I have placed it here for the following reason. Unless a teacher is able to tap into his or her own personal higher order thinking skills in response to the demands of unique academic tasks (i.e., to be strategic oneself), that teacher will be unable to teach students the strategies they need. Teaching students how and when to use cognitive strategies is a vastly different enterprise than drilling students on a discrete skill or serving up a smorgasbord of content and expecting students to discover and construct their own knowledge. Strategic teaching takes thought.

Attempting to teach content to students, however, without simultaneously providing cognitive-strategy instruction is like offering food to hungry diners but failing to provide them with the necessary dinnerware. The skillful union of content and strategy instruction is a powerful aid to learning, a marriage that should delight all content-area teachers who love their discipline and want every student to appreciate and master it. There are two catches, however. "Becoming an effective . . . strategies instruction teacher takes several years" (Brown et al., 1996, p. 20; Irene Gaskins, personal communication, July 5, 2000). Moreover, most students require four to nine class sessions to learn a strategy well enough to use it independently (Harris & Graham, 1996).

Mike Simmons is a strategic teacher. At the beginning of each school year, he introduces his freshman World History students to the concept of strategic reading. He asks them: "What do effective readers actually do when they read? What habits make them able to comprehend, analyze, and interpret a text? How do they make sense of challenging material?"

After a brief discussion, he models strategic reading and thinking for his students. To do this he reads aloud from an unfamiliar (to both him and his students) challenging text. His choice for the lesson we are observing is the preface to Immanuel Kant's *Critique of Pure Reason* (1907). Mr. Simmons is reading aloud when we slip into the classroom. During his reading, he frequently thinks aloud, pausing to question, reflect, paraphrase, reread, and look back. Students hear him articulate what is going through his mind. He asked the students to take notes during his reading, not on the content of the text, but rather on his efforts to gain meaning from what he reads. After approximately 5 minutes of reading aloud alternated with thinking aloud, the class generates a list of Mr. Simmons's thoughts and behaviors.

After Mr. Simmons and his students talk about the list they have generated, he gives them a brief reading assignment and then asks them to think aloud with a partner after reading it. During his yearlong World History course he will not only teach the required content, he will also teach his students how to organize, understand, learn, and remember the content in more efficient and effective ways. He will teach one strategy at a time, introducing a new one only when his students are well on their way to mastering the previous one. He will continue to model the use of all of the strategies for his students, but will gradually expect them to choose appropriate ones for use on their own. His goal is to help students understand and remember the content of his course in more effective ways than they would have if taught through typical lectures and class discussions (M. Arest, personal communication, June, 2000).

Every classroom teacher must be a strategic teacher—proficient at providing explicit cognitive-strategy instruction to students. Explicit instruction includes modeling, explaining, providing practice, giving feedback, supplying the rationale for choosing a given strategy, and demonstrating the specific settings in which the strategy is most applicable.[2] Highly effective teachers are strategic—not only in their personal learning lives, but also in the ways they teach cognitive strategies to students.

Reflective

> *Reflecting on teaching and reflecting on one's self is not common. It is not sufficiently encouraged in preparation programs or in inservice education. Instead, there is ingrained in many teachers the need to be "doers" and persons of action.*
>
> Dollase (1992, p. 89)

Reflection is the examination of one's teaching practice in a thoughtful and even critical way, learning from this process, and then using what has been learned to affect one's future action. Reflection is about making sense of one's professional life. Self-reflection is not for the faint of heart. I know. I reflect on my practice after every workshop I do. I am fortunate to have a partner with whom to reflect, my husband, who assists me. However, even when done with a caring and loving person, self-examination can be painful. I struggle to adjust the balance between content and process, fine-tune my instructional flow, and think about how I could have done a better job of meeting the needs of my diverse audience. I know that "activity not checked by observation and analysis may be enjoyable, but intellectually it usually goes nowhere, neither to greater clarification nor to new ideas and experience" (Chickering, 1977, p. 18). I know that reflection is difficult work, but it is one of the most productive ways in which a teacher can spend time.

Reflection as discussed in this section is different from what teachers do during the act of teaching as they fine-tune and make adjustments on the spur of the moment. Reflection in this context has to do with a more substantive kind of thought process—one that examines values and poses difficult questions:

1. What is my teaching like?

2. Why is it like this?

3. How has it come to be this way?

4. What are the effects of my teaching on my students?

5. What would I like to improve and why?

6. How can I improve what I do? (Ghaye & Ghaye, 1998, pp. 20, 67)

Reflection is more than just thinking and then talking about that thinking. Reflection is a creative process that demands change, improvement, and movement. Reflection should be "formative, that is periodic, constructive, and deliberate" (Valverde, 1982, p. 86). Highly effective teachers know the value of reflection, are willing to invest the energy it requires, have the courage it takes to bare one's soul to one's self and others, and commit to action as a result of what they uncover in their thinking.

Communicative

Communication often follows a period of reflection. To be communicative as a teacher is to be able to articulate ideas, issues, beliefs, and values about teaching and learning with colleagues, students, and parents in an artful and clear fashion. Several of the highly effective teachers who contributed to this book regularly communicate their ideas, beliefs, and values about teaching and education, not only to their school communities, but also to public audiences. Donna Garner (1997), Carol Jago (2000,

2001), Jerry Jesness (1998, 1999, 2000a, 2000b), and Linda Taylor (1995, 2001) are all published authors. They write columns, op-ed pieces, books, articles, and curricula. To write is to wrestle with ideas, come to grips with what one really believes, and even to be subjected to criticism or a measure of professional notoriety. Other highly effective teachers like Adrienne Hamparian Johnson and Carol Reimann regularly give workshops in their own districts and around their states. Communicative teachers are able to examine provocative issues and problems, discuss them from a variety of perspectives, and articulate their beliefs and values about them in a public forum—whether that be a faculty gathering, a board of education meeting, or a letter to the editor. Less effective teachers communicate in the parking lot, in the teachers' lounge, and behind closed doors.

Responsive

Few teachers finish their careers in the same school or even the same district in which they began teaching. Many change subjects or grade levels many times. Some move to other states or even exchange teaching positions with their counterparts around the world. Highly effective teachers are responsive: able to flex to the changing needs and demands of the profession.

Jerry Jesness has taught in a variety of unique and challenging settings during his teaching career. There was the Crazy Horse School on the Pine Ridge Reservation in South Dakota; a "blackboard jungle" school where he served as an ESL teacher; and his current assignment in Los Fresnos, Texas, where he is a special-education teacher working with bilingual students. Jerry is an out-of-field teacher, never having taken a college course in special or elementary education. He did his student teaching at an international school in the Canary Islands and along the way picked up an MA in Spanish literature. He is the personification of flex, artfully adapting to each new situation and loving it.

Highly effective teachers adapt to new principals, new superintendents, boundary changes, remodeling projects, curricular upheaval, lack of materials, lack of money, lack of instructional leadership, innovations too numerous to mention, loss of jobs, loss of face, angry parents, violent students, reassignments, relocations, grade changes, subject changes, room changes, budget cuts, school closings, school openings, school board elections, and mind-numbing tragedies with equanimity. They come to work through snowstorms, earthquakes, mud slides, and floods.

They show up with broken legs, cancer, toothaches, and in labor. They walk, drive hundreds of miles, ride their bikes, take the train, and even fly to get to school. They teach through jackhammers, bitter cold, suffocating heat, falling asbestos, peeling paint, and broken toilets. They teach without textbooks, library books, and sometimes even paper and pencils. Highly effective teachers are the most amazing people I know. They are as flexible as slinky toys when it comes to adjusting to the demands the profession lays upon them. Yet, they remain firm as the rock of Gibraltar when it comes to their values and beliefs.

Get a Life—A Mental Life

This final trait of highly effective teachers is no less important for being last on our list. Unfortunately, some teachers have adopted a stance of anti-intellectualism that is discouraging, not only to the public at large, but to their colleagues who do recognize and appreciate how much highly effective teachers must know to effectively do the job of teaching. Figure 6.1 (found earlier in this chapter) summarizes the various aspects of the intellectual traits that demonstrate knowledge, curiosity, and awareness.

Recapping the Ten Traits of Highly Effective Teachers

Learning theory shows that students tend to remember items at the beginning and the end of a list more readily than items that occur in the middle (Saphier & Gower, 1997). This principle likely holds true for ideas found at the beginnings and endings of books as well. You can no doubt more readily recall one of the personal traits you read about earlier in Chapter 2 than you can the teaching traits that were tucked in the middle of the book. I'm also confident that one of the final traits we just discussed is also right on the tip of your tongue.

If I could choose only two traits from my list of 10 to have you retain in your long-term memory and then retrieve the next time you're ready to hire a teacher, I would choose Traits 2 (Positive and Real) and either 8 (Book Learning) or 10 (A Mental Life). In Chapter 7 you will formally meet Alan Jones, a high school principal, who shares his perspective on interviewing and hiring teachers for his very diverse, but award-winning high school. You'll discover that Alan only looks for two things when he hires teachers: how they feel about students and can interact with them (Trait 2) and their mastery of subject matter and intellectual capabilities (Traits 8 and 10).

Marsha Arest concurs. In one of our many conversations about teaching she asked if I'd ever heard the saying, "It's not how much you know, but how much you care." Of course I had. It's been around for a long time. The idea is that if you like kids, you'll make a good teacher. Marsha was adamant about her disagreement with the statement, however. "I don't buy it because I think a teacher needs to have that content and knowledge piece." "But," she went on to say, "trust me, if there isn't any 'caring,' then the knowledge will never be transmitted."

Which traits do you think are most important? Do the teachers you hire reflect the importance you place on the various traits? Which traits do you think your teachers value most about themselves? About their colleagues? About you as an administrator? Which traits do you think the parents of your community would select as most important in the individuals who teach their children? You don't have to answer these questions right now, but as an educator, you can't postpone dealing with them indefinitely. If you're a principal, the answers will drive your teacher-selection and staff-development processes. If you're a teacher, the answers to these questions will drive your own personal quest to become a highly effective teacher.

Looking Ahead

In the chapters ahead, we move our focus from the 10 traits to consider the practicalities of staffing a school in Chapter 7, ensuring that new teachers have the tools and support to become effective in their own right in Chapter 8, and finally to empowering and energizing experienced teachers in Chapter 9.

Notes

1. The Ball Foundation Parent Involvement Program (Glen Ellyn, IL) began as a way to find out what effect parent involvement had on student achievement. Teachers who volunteer to be in the program offer a fall home visit to any child whose parent(s) or guardians wish to participate. Each visit lasts approximately 20 min. In the spring, a phone confer-

ence is offered to any family who wishes to participate. The program has grown each year since its inception and currently has volunteer teachers from all five elementary buildings. At the beginning of the 2000-2001 school year, a pilot program was begun at the middle school. Direct phone service is installed and phones are purchased by the Foundation for the classrooms of the volunteer teachers. Stipends are paid to the teachers by the school district. Teachers may opt in or out of the program each year. About 70 teachers per year participate.

2. This description of strategic teaching is adapted by permission from McEwan, Elaine K. (2001). *Raising Reading Achievement in Middle and High Schools: Five Simple-to-Follow Strategies for Principals.* Thousand Oaks, CA: Corwin Press.

7

Hiring Highly Effective Teachers

I'm not quite a teacher yet—that is, I haven't had a class of my own. That's in September, if I last and if the new school opens on time. I'm surprised Mr. Turner hired me, only twenty-four years old, to help him open a brand-new public school. You would think he would want someone more experienced. The interview was very brief. He asked, "How would you describe your classroom discipline style?"

I answered, "Assertive."

He said, "What does that mean?"

"It means I say what I mean and I mean what I say," I replied.

"Well say you're having a problem with a student, how would you deal with it?"

"I would document the child's behavior and then try interventions such as using successive approximations toward our goal or home involvement, depending on the individual situation," I explained. After a silence, I added, "I wouldn't call the office every five minutes."

He closed the little notebook on his lap and announced, "You're hired."

Codell (1999, pp. 3-4)

A Good Teacher Is Hard to Find

Signing bonuses. Housing perks. Bidding wars. We're not talking Silicon Valley or big-league baseball here. We're talking teaching. The list of enticements being offered by states and districts desperate to hire teachers is dazzling to those of us who had to pound the pavement to find our first jobs: student loan-forgiveness programs, moving assistance, free graduate courses, bonuses for earned certification from the National Board for Professional Teaching Standards, and even low-interest mortgages and down-payment assistance (Galley, 2001). Math and science teachers are at a premium. Bilingual and special education teachers are being snapped up like blue-light specials at Kmart. Minority teachers are almost impossible to find. Principals who aren't on their toes may just find that one of their star teachers has been recruited by a megadistrict with a Madison Avenue advertising budget.

Demographers are estimating that schools will need to hire two million public school teachers in the first 10 years of the new millennium, leaving many administrators scrambling to find warm bodies to fill their classrooms. Even after they've hired them, there are no guarantees that the best teachers will remain. Of those who begin teaching, about one in five leaves after three years in the classroom. Unfortunately, those most likely to leave are the teachers who were the top undergraduates as measured by their scores on college entrance exams (Olson, 2000). Teacher shortages don't affect every administrator, however. Sharon Huffman is a principal in Hinsdale, Illinois, where there are hundreds of applicants for every teaching vacancy. Her district has an outstanding K-8 teacher compensation package and is willing to pay for master's degrees and up to five years of experience. Hiring the best and the brightest in Hinsdale is easier than in many places. The same is true in the Rockwood School District (MO). Jan Antrim has only hired one novice teacher in her 10 years in Rockwood: "We have the luxury of having countless experienced teachers applying to our district and the support of a board of education that doesn't force us to hire inexperienced people."

Administrators who work in urban or rural areas, districts with marginal salary schedules, or locations where population growth is exploding exponentially, are not as fortunate as Jan Antrim and Sharon Huffman. Rural and urban administrators must be creative, aggressive, and sometimes downright sneaky to find the teachers they need. Recruiters in the Chicago Public Schools are selling prospective teachers on the amenities to be found in big-city life, recruiting overseas teachers, and establishing their own student-teaching programs with state universities (Johnston, 2000). Some states are calling back retired teachers to work in critical-need areas, waiving the usual restrictions imposed on teaching while drawing a teachers' pension (Blair, 1999). Some recruiters are targeting teachers in specific schools by word of mouth, advertising in local newspapers, and placing ads on radio stations (Blair, 2000).

Experienced principals are exercising all of their options:

1. Asking current staff members if they have relatives or friends who are looking for teaching opportunities

2. Persuading aides, substitutes, paraprofessionals, or parents who have certificates to consider full-time positions

3. Suggesting that a current faculty member earn certification in a specialty area (e.g., the library, special education, or speech pathology)

4. Aggressively recruiting student-teacher placements in their buildings

5. Placing advertisements on Web sites and in newspapers

6. Encouraging staff members on maternity leave to consider job sharing rather than resigning completely

7. Sharing job applications with other districts

8. Working with colleges to offer special certification programs in-district

9. Building relationships with placement officers and department chairpersons at universities to identify outstanding candidates

Hiring the Best and the Brightest: A Panel Discussion

Once you have a stack of applications in hand, what steps should you take to select the most effective teachers for your vacancies? I have assembled a panel of experienced principals to describe the process in their schools. They are knowledgeable, skilled, and eager to share their expertise with fellow educators. If you are a principal preparing for the spring roundup of candidates, or if you are a teacher preparing for that all-important job interview, you will enjoy eavesdropping as these principals "talk shop" about hiring teachers.

Introducing the Panel

Elaine: Panel members, please introduce yourselves to our readers. We'll go in alphabetical order.

Sandra Ahola: I'm the principal of Pomfret Community School (CT). My school is PreK–Grade 8 and has 535 students. I've worked in the building for 22 years—as a guidance counselor, director of special services, assistant principal, and for the last 5 years as principal. I guess that's an upwardly mobile path!

Jan Antrim: I'm the principal of Eureka School in the Rockwood School (MO) District in suburban St. Louis (Eureka School). We have 270 wonderful, shining little Wildcats and 13 fabulous, dedicated and talented classroom teachers. I am finishing my 14th glorious year as a building principal.

Gregg Garman: I'm the headmaster of Mercer Christian Academy, a K-12 school in Ewing, New Jersey. We have 225 students from a variety of ethnic and socioeconomic backgrounds who are taught by a staff of 24. I'm in my 2nd year here.

Sharon Huffman: I've been the principal at The Lane School, a K-5 building in Hinsdale, Illinois, for 8 years. We have 327 students taught by 25 teachers, including the specials and resource teachers.

Alan Jones: Every high school possesses a culture—a distinct theme that one feels in the hallways and when talking with teachers. The distinct theme that runs through the hallways of Community High School, a very diverse high school in the far western suburbs of Chicago, is its focus on the classroom teacher. While other principals in the area spend time developing different types of schedules, or developing a mission statement, or the implementation of a new program (e.g., "Character Counts," "Assertive Discipline," "Authentic Assessment"), I have allocated time and resources to frequent observation and coaching of classroom instruction and the professional development of teachers. Every department in our school has staff members who are regular presenters at conferences, others authored textbooks and articles in professional journals, and many have become leaders in various in-house staff development efforts. Most importantly, the culture of our building—what is the most important thing we do—has remained in the classroom.

Kathy Miller: Prairie Oaks School is part of the College Community School District in Cedar Rapids, Iowa. It is a segregated facility housed on the Four Oaks Residential Treatment Center campus. We have close to 50 students, all of whom are severely behavior disordered. In addition to serving as principal of Prairie Oaks, I also am the Director of Special Education for the District. I've been here for almost 4 years.

John Patterson: I'm the principal of Hawthorne School in Wheaton, Illinois. I've been a principal for 12 years. Hawthorne is a K-5 school with 300 students.

Sally Roth: I've been the principal of Meadowlawn School in Perkins, Ohio, for 9 years. We have 530 students, Grades two through five, and a teaching staff of 36. In addition to our many self-contained classrooms, we also have six multi-age classrooms. The teachers in these classrooms have trained over 3 years to create a blended community of learners, implement continuous improvement and provide individualized goal attainment. I've been an educator for over 30 years and have been a principal for almost half of that time.

The Importance of Hiring the Best

Elaine: Of all of the things you do as a principal, where does interviewing and hiring teachers fit in?

Sally Roth: I look at the interview process as a professional development activity for our school. The hiring of quality people for teaching positions is a key way in which a school evolves and improves. I find the interviewing and selection process to be the most important work I do for students because it has the greatest impact upon them. Whomever we select becomes the teacher our students live with for one school year. That person can change lives.

Sandra Ahola: Interviewing and selecting teachers is the most important thing I do as an administrator. I never take this task lightly because I am anticipating the future and I don't have the luxury of making mistakes.

John Patterson: I agree. Hiring is one of a principal's most important jobs. Selecting the people who will work with kids is key to a school's success.

Getting Started

Elaine: When you determine that you have a vacancy, how do you get the process under way?

Sandra Ahola: I get right down to work the minute I know there will be an opening. I always do some in-house advertising first. You never know what kind of goodies you might uncover regarding teachers who want to switch schools. I give priority consideration to in-house applicants as they have lots to offer. An administrator needs to know where people belong in a system and this is a role I love playing.

John Patterson: We have a two-part screening process that takes place at central office. The candidates who pass a paper screening are then given a phone or face-to-face interview. If they make the grade a second time, they are added to a computer database that principals can access whenever they have a vacancy. Ideally, I can go to my computer, plug in the information that I'm looking for, say a primary teacher with 3 to 5 years of experience, and I'll be given a list of candidates who have been prescreened and approved. The computer doesn't always give me what I ask for, but it's a good start. We can also interview people who have been substitutes or aides in our buildings.

Alan Jones: As soon as we know a teacher is needed, the Human Resources person and I sit down with the department chair and develop a "profile" of the teacher we need. We look at the types of courses this teacher will have to teach. If we're hiring a math

** STARBUCKS COFFEE COMPANY **

SHADLE PARK CENTE   #08681
SPOKANE   WA99205

1 VT BREWED COFFEE   1.85
SUBTOTAL   1.85
  TAX 8.6   0.16
TOTAL   2.01
CASH   2.01
CHANGE DUE   0.00

08681 03A1 700042 001569846E
07/10/08   08:09
BRING THIS RECEIPT BACK TODAY
to select SPOK store after 1pm
for $1 off any size cold drink
One per customer w purchase
prior to 1 pm Value 1/2 cent

TREAT RECEIPT
Bring this in after 1pm today,
and get $1 off any cold drink.

teacher, we want that person to have advanced geometry and differential equations on the transcript. If we're hiring someone to teach American History, I want to see a solid core of upper-level courses in that department. Sometimes I'll bring up other concerns I personally might have, such as whether we need a teacher in this department who speaks Spanish, but the profile is really up to the department chairperson. I know that in many high schools in our area, principals try to fit a coaching position in with a teaching position, and I just won't do that. I'm looking for the very best teacher. Coaching would not be a high priority in the decision. Once we've developed a profile, then the HR person begins to look at applications. I'll be frank—we look at grade point averages, the number of higher level courses the applicant has taken in his discipline, and the university that granted the degree. The HR person will usually give 3 to 5 applications to the department chair who will then come back with the 2 to 3 he or she wants to interview.

Sharon Huffman: The interview process in our district begins with the Director of Human Resources. Her office sends out applications that contain four key questions to which applicants must respond with short essay answers. The director then selects candidates to call in for a screening interview. I receive the names of the approved applicants, usually 10 to 12 individuals who are a possible fit for my posted teaching position and I then select five to call in for an hour-long interview with a team of teachers.

Jan Antrim: When I review applications, I look at the variety of experience, the quality of the written portion to assess writing skills, and for respected references and education.

Gregg Garman: Our school is privileged to be in an area of numerous quality higher education institutions. They often place their student teachers in the building. These opportunities allow us to get to know prospective teachers firsthand. When we see excellent prospects, we strongly encourage them to apply for open positions at our school. I also make frequent calls to these institutions for names of possible teachers for openings we may have. As resumes and applications are received, I distribute them to my administrative team for their input. Once strong candidates are identified, an initial interview is arranged and references are checked.

Teachers Hiring Teachers

Elaine: Who participates in your interviewing process?

Sharon Huffman: The makeup of the teacher team is dependent on the position—teachers at the grade level where the opening occurs, one teacher from the grade ahead, one teacher from the grade below, and one teacher from the special areas of art, music, physical education, or learning disabilities resource.

Gregg Garman: Our interview team has been a tremendous help in this process. The team usually has four or five members made up of teachers, administrators, and parents. The team will be the same for all of the candidates for an open position, but there may be several teams meeting depending on the number of vacancies.

Sally Roth: I try to give all of the teachers in the school an opportunity to serve on an interview team at one time or another. This gives them a vested interest in the later success of the new hire.

Sandra Ahola: I establish a team of from four to eight teachers. I am a member of this team—a peer, not the leader. Teachers do at times tend to defer to me, and I have to be conscious of this so that I'm not driving their decisions.

John Patterson: I see it as a win-win situation for both administrators and teachers when they work as a team to hire new people. It's an education for the teachers as well. Sometimes they'll get an "aha" during an interview that will result in their doing something different in their own classroom. I tell the teacher team that they are there to give me input and to provide another lens through which to view the candidate, but the ultimate selection is mine.

Alan Jones: We're a bit different in that we're a one high school district and have a very streamlined process. The interview team consists of the HR person, the department chair, a teacher if it's a team assignment, and me.

Popping the Questions

Elaine: Where do you get your interview questions?

Sandra Ahola: I have a database of questions in my computer. I've developed it over the years and it includes questions I've picked up at different conferences as well as some that teachers have generated. I try to choose questions that will give us an all-around picture of the applicant and provide opportunities for more in-depth discussion, as well as follow-up questions. The questions are definitely important; there certainly have been times when I felt an interview was "flat," not necessarily because of the person, but because of the particular questions that were asked.

Alan Jones: There are really just two basic questions that I need to have answered in the interview process. Does the person have a deep understanding of his or her subject? Does the person like kids? Usually the department chair handles the content piece. One question that we often use comes out of the recent national discussions about U.S. math curriculum—"a mile wide and an inch deep." We'll ask, "If you had to get rid of three topics in your discipline (e.g., algebra, biology, American history), what would they be?" Another related question we might ask is "Name one topic in your discipline that you would die for." The basic question is "What knowledge is of most worth to you?" The HR person handles the second part of the interview and that focuses on how the applicant feels about kids and how he or she will relate to kids. She'll describe some different classroom scenarios to the candidate and ask how he or she would handle them.

Sally Roth: The team and I meet to discuss what needs and philosophy will drive the interview process. We create and assign questions for the interview based on what we are looking for in a candidate. For example, we may need a grade-five traditional teacher. Or, we may need a grade 4/5 multi-age teacher. There is a difference in the kind of skills necessary for each position. We keep these criteria in mind when creating questions. We always include questions regarding differentiation of instruction, how a person relates to children and to parents, and what they believe about giftedness and also about learning disabilities.

John Patterson: We get our questions from a yellow folder. I've been a principal for thirteen years and since my very first teacher interview I've saved every question I've ever used, either alone or with a team. It's a hodgepodge of other principals' questions, questions

my teachers have suggested, as well as questions my superintendent asked when we did interviews together when I first became an
administrator. I always manage to find just the right questions in
my yellow folder.

That Special Question

Elaine: Are there any unique or special questions you ask each
candidate?

Kathy Miller: We ask what books a candidate has read recently and
which books have been the most influential with respect to student
learning and achievement. If the candidate is in the field of special
education, we ask about their knowledge of the law and their ability to write good IEPs.

John Patterson: One question we frequently use in our interviews is
"What is your passion?" During one of my earliest interviews with
a team of teachers, a first-grade teacher suggested this question. It's
been a winner ever since.

Jan Antrim: We ask candidates for specific examples of how he or
she has reacted in the past to certain situations. "Tell me about a
time when you . . . "

Gregg Garman: We use a standard set of interview questions and
rating form that each team member completes after the interview.
But we also have a list of supplementary questions that have
proven to be quite helpful in getting at the critical attributes of a
candidate. These are questions I've collected over the years from
various teachers and administrators with whom I've worked.

- What do you hope to accomplish as a teacher?

- How do you find out about your students' attitudes and feelings about your class?

- Do you teach with an overall plan in mind for the year or would
  you rather teach some interesting things and let the process determine the results?

What to Look For in the Interview

Elaine: What are you essentially looking for during the interview process? The "big picture," if you will?

Sally Roth: The purpose of the interview is to delve deeply and get the person to show his or her true colors, demonstrate consistency, and reveal some spark of enthusiasm and truth that cannot be denied. We are looking for a good person first and skilled teacher, second.

John Patterson: I ask very open-ended kinds of questions—things like "Tell me about reading and language arts instruction." I want teachers who can give me the "gestalt" of a curricular area without any prompting. I rely on the candidate to come in and essentially unpack their briefcase or backpack of knowledge and show us what they have.

Sharon Huffman: In hearing candidates' responses I listen for child focus, a sense of child development, a knowledge of related curriculum in general, and a knowledge of varied instructional strategies. I listen for a sense of "giftedness as a teacher" within the responses of the candidate—a "with-it-ness," a connectedness, a wholesomeness which accompanies perceived competence in elementary education. If a candidate volunteers to talk about how he or she always liked to play school or teach younger brothers and sisters, I have found that to be a good indication of success. The evidence of a sense of humor is essential.

Sandra Ahola: During the interview we're looking for connections with people, team work, love and more love of children (absolutely essential), knowledge of the profession, commitment to excellence in education, flexibility. This person also needs to have an overall fit with the position—whether it's working closely with two other teachers in 8th grade or a specialist's area where he or she must deal with 45 teachers and 530 students every week. The personality has to fit.

Alan Jones: I'm looking for someone who has thought deeply about his or her discipline. If I ask, "What topic currently taught in U.S. History would you throw out as superfluous to the curriculum?" and the candidate says, "That's an interesting question. I've never thought about it," my antennae go up. I'm always looking for brilliance or genius in a teacher, but I'm realistic enough to know that I may have to settle for a little less than that on most occasions—and hire what I call a "meat and potatoes" teacher. A good solid teacher that's going to get the job done.

Performance-Based Assessments

Elaine: What other kinds of information do you ask for in addition to the interview?

Jan Antrim: I ask candidates to bring along a portfolio—something to "knock my socks off." We also ask candidates to teach a 5-minute lesson. We give them 5 minutes to prepare and then after they teach for 5 minutes, we ask them how they would finish the lesson. If a candidate is currently student teaching or teaching in another location, I always arrange to visit his or her classroom and observe a lesson.

Kathy Miller: We ask for a writing sample so we can judge the candidate's writing ability. We also ask the candidate to teach a lesson to a group of students in the building. We have summer school, so even then we have students available. I sit in on this lesson and watch the person. I evaluate what they choose to teach, how they present the lesson, how good their classroom management is, how they handle disruptive students, and how they relate and interact with students. I also like to observe candidates interacting with the staff in the teacher work area.

Alan Jones: More and more candidates are bringing in portfolios and videotapes and I always gratefully accept everything they bring in. I usually take it home, watch the video, and go through the portfolio very carefully. I had a principal colleague say to me not long ago, "But you're just seeing their best work." I thought that was the whole idea. If this is their best, then I have a pretty good idea of the kind of quality I'll see from this teacher in the classroom.

Gregg Garman: We use a variety of probes for the writing samples. For example, we might ask the candidate to assume he or she has just been hired to replace someone who resigned suddenly and to write an introductory letter to the parents introducing him- or herself and making them feel more comfortable with him or her as their child's new teacher. Another question we might use to elicit a writing sample is: "What personal characteristics do you possess that will lead to a successful experience in your role as an educator at our school?"

Making the Final Decision

Elaine: Describe the final process when you make your decision.

Alan Jones: Between the three of us—the HR person, the department chair, and I—we know what we want, and it doesn't take us long to know whether or not we've found it. "Has the candidate thought reflectively about his or her subject matter and does the candidate like high school kids?" I can coach someone on classroom management and discipline techniques if they need help in those areas, but if the candidate has no idea what's important in his or her discipline and can't make sense of that for kids, I can't help them.

Sharon Huffman: After an interview, each teacher on the team, without talking to anyone else on the team, writes a response on a sheet that I provide. I endeavor to avoid "group think." At the end of all the interviews for an identified position, I ask each teacher on the interview team to rank order his or her choices and write a rationale for selecting the top two candidates. Then I put the teachers' selections all together to see who is our number one candidate. Often we discuss the candidates' strengths and weaknesses in light of the "best fit" for our faculty team. I lay the ground rule that although I want the teachers' input and I value it, the final decision for the person to be selected is mine because I am finally responsible for the supervision of the new teacher. In 8 years I've never had to contradict the final recommendation from the teachers.

Sandra Ahola: The actual process of selecting the finalists is fascinating. It can also be brutal as we are painfully honest; within strict professional parameters we are open in our frankness about candidates and we look at our system realistically, knowing the strengths and weaknesses. People have told us that our standards were tough, that it was hard to get a job here, but that it was so worth the effort. Some have gone through the process two or three times before being hired.

John Patterson: We debrief after every interview and when we're finished with all of them, I ask the team members to list the top three people with whom they could live. Most of the time we're all in agreement. If for any reason there are some doubts or disagreements, I bring the top people back for a second interview to ask some follow-up questions.

Sally Roth: We actually do two sets of interviews. After the first interview, we all write a number from 1 to 3 on the notes we make, for future reference. When all the candidates have been interviewed, the team and I meet for lunch and compare notes, along with our rating for each person. We explain why we rated the candidate the way we did. I then disclose my ratings after the team members have revealed their scores. We seldom disagree. Then we decide on two or three candidates to bring back for a final interview. We probe the candidate for more specifics in this second interview. The team is going to have to market this person to the rest of the staff. If I, as building principal, do not agree with the final choice, I will say so and will express why I feel this way. However, I have never found the team to select a teacher I couldn't support.

Hiring the Wrong Person

Elaine: Do you ever make mistakes?

John Patterson: Although I've done a lot of interviewing—I hired 40 teachers in seven years at one school, which adds up to more than 320 interviews overall—it's not one of my favorite things to do. It's so time-consuming and sometimes I just have to force myself to sit down and do it. But I've been very fortunate. The one area where we've had a problem or two was when a new hire was really good with kids, wonderful with parents, but couldn't get along with the other staff members. That never came out anywhere in the interview. Those are hard situations to handle—especially in a school where the people who are already there really work together well.

Kathy Miller: I haven't made many mistakes yet but I've only been doing this a few years. If we have a position open and the candidate pool is poor we do not fill the position with just any warm body. We go with a long-term sub (up to one-half of the year) and continue looking for a suitable person for the job. Many districts get in a rush in late July or in August because they don't have a position filled—especially in special education—and so they hire a person who they normally wouldn't and get into lots of problems both legally and with the person's ability to do a good job. Many people still do not call references and if they did they would not hire the person. We always call three references and have a standard list of questions we ask. We don't fill the position unless we think the person is the best we can get for the job. When we do make a mistake, we spend a lot of time with the person doing observations, meeting with the person, and outlining expectations and giving timelines for changes as a part of our intensive remediation system. If the person is not able to make the necessary changes in the appropriate time frame, we ask for their resignation.

Jan Antrim: I have been very fortunate to have the opportunity to observe many of the candidates in their classrooms. Our district calls for retirements and resignations in April though teachers do have until July 1. The April date gives me plenty of time to make observations. I have only hired one inexperienced teacher in my 10 years here in Rockwood. We have the luxury of having countless experienced teachers applying to our district and the support of a board of education that doesn't force us to hire inexperienced teachers just to save money. During the summer months, I can sometimes observe candidates if they are working at a daycare or teaching summer school; however, I am less likely to get a visit in during the summer. Some of my colleagues ask teachers to come in and teach a minilesson during the interview, but I love to actually see the teacher in action. I can't tell you how many times I've seen a teacher be great in the interview and then I'm shocked to see the lack of words being put into action in the classroom. As for mistakes in hiring, I have been very fortunate. In our district, we are encouraged to do our weeding in the first year. We can typically "nonrenew" a nontenured teacher pretty easily in the first year. All that said, I haven't had to do that. I did have a librarian who didn't work out well and she chose to take another position when she was told she would not be renewed. I worked with her intensely throughout the year, but she wasn't showing any improvement.

Sandra Ahola: Molding new teachers is a tough job, especially if they don't arrive with the basic skills and attitudes. If that's the case, difficult decisions must be made and the sooner the better. I don't believe that everyone can teach! Some personality issues and true feelings for children cannot be taught or learned in a short period of time. Schools are under tremendous pressure to achieve and excel every day. We don't have time to "fix" borderline new teachers. Somehow they got farther than they should have and it's time to call it quits. I try to nonrenew such teachers after the very first year, rather than prolonging the agony. I give it my all, do my observations, give feedback on my honest perceptions, and if I don't see the right changes quickly, I move the case on. Don't get me wrong; this is an emotional and draining issue for all the staff. Somehow they feel like they have failed and that everyone can be fixed (since they believe that for all children) and it's hard for them to agree that we need to part with some teachers. They definitely fall apart, become anxious—even paranoid—thinking their jobs are on the line. The trust factor between staff/administration suffers immediately. It does get better but the most important job is hiring the right person and doing it the first time around! I feel good about the people that I have hired; the problems that have arisen tend to be based on personal situations that evolved with the employee later on. The most obvious problem hires were due to lack of qualified candidates, and decisions made based on expediency and not on quality.

Gregg Garman: Do I make mistakes in hiring? Oh yes! But not as many as I used to. The best time to release someone is during the interview process—before you hire them. When a mistake is made, we try to work with the teacher or staff member in order to correct deficiencies. In the private school setting (at least with our school), contracts are signed on a yearly basis. Sometimes we handle it by personally talking with the individual to encourage them to improve or help them see that the position is not a fit for them. Sometimes the person will resign after realizing this. If the mistake involves a teacher who refuses constructive feedback and mentoring help, then we begin the due process of releasing that teacher especially if this person is a detriment to the students in his or her class.

In any of the mistakes that have been made in hiring, I always attempt to give the person ample opportunities to improve and prove us wrong. Sometimes a teacher will realize on his or her own that the fit is not a good one, or that teaching is not for him or her, and ask to be released from the teaching position. My desire is to have a smooth transition when we have to release someone. Communication with the individual as well as the school community is important so that the least possible disruption occurs. Many of my former mistakes in hiring have been eliminated because of the use of an interview team in the screening process.

Interview Questions.

One important aspect of interviewing teacher candidates has to do with asking the right questions—questions that will disclose the person behind the application and reveal the characteristics and traits that you and your team want to see in the teachers you hire. Resource C contains over 50 interview questions—several for each of the 10 traits we identified throughout the book. You can use the list in its entirety or pick and choose questions to integrate into your current interview format.

Recapping Chapter 7

Choosing teachers in today's schools is a team effort. Principals have learned to share the decision making, and the benefits are many:

1. Staff members feel vested in the process and are more willing to support and encourage someone they helped to choose.

2. Staff members learn and grow professionally through their participation, gaining an appreciation for the process, and an introduction to new methods and perspectives from the various candidates.

3. Staff members become aware of the importance of building a team that can work together to achieve building improvement goals.

Looking Ahead

Hiring the best possible candidates for your teaching vacancies is only the beginning. The "care and feeding" of new teachers is an important undertaking for you and your staff. Of those individuals who begin teaching in any given year, about one in five leaves after three years in the classroom (Olson, 2000), many because they did not receive the support they needed to become successful. Chapter 8 gives you several dozen ideas of things you can do with brand-new teachers to make them feel welcome and to help them become highly effective teachers.

8

Mentoring
New Teachers

How to Retain the
Effective Teachers You Hire

My principal utilizes a great deal of informal coaching and mentoring. He is in and out of the entire faculty's classes. I value his insights because he was an excellent teacher. His love of children and young people was so obvious that we trusted him somehow. . . . Often he asks if he could teach a class. Watching him is a joy. I honestly believe I did some of my best reflecting after talking with him or watching this man teach.

Blase and Blase (1998, pp. 40-41)

Did you have a mentor when you began teaching? I certainly didn't. It was "sink or swim." Sometimes I felt a lot like Robinson Crusoe, Daniel Defoe's heroic survivor, or if you prefer a more contemporary survivor, Tom Hanks. Dan Lortie observes that, like Defoe's hero, the beginning teacher may find that prior excellence supplied him with some alternatives for action, but his crucial learning comes from his personal errors; he fits together solutions and specific problems into some kind of whole and at times finds leeway for the expression of personal tastes. Working largely alone, he cannot make the specifics of his working knowledge base explicit, nor need he, as his victories are private. (1966, p. 59)

Although "the beginning teacher pipeline is riddled with leaks and faulty filters" (Boser, 2000, p. 17), an increasing number of new teachers no longer have to endure a "trial by fire," a "rite of passage," or their own personal version of *Survivor* to make it through the first year of teaching. Many states have mandated mentoring programs (e.g., Connecticut, Missouri, and Ohio). There are a variety of well-developed models that districts can adopt to provide ongoing help for beginning teachers— whether it's called mentoring, coaching, assisting, or supporting. These programs don't come without a cost, however, but a sizable up-front investment in new teachers will save time and money in the long run. Boser (2000) reports that teachers who did not participate in an induction program in their schools or districts were nearly twice as likely to leave the classroom (20%) as those who participated in such a program (11%).

Induction is loosely defined by some to be "the entry of individuals to the teaching profession" (Brock & Grady, 1997, p. 8). In some districts, the entry is swift and short, one or two days of orientation, a three-ring binder filled with policies and forms—and new teachers are out on their own. Orientation is generally considered to be a collection of sessions devoted to giving teachers the critical information they need to be immediately successful—what to do if they suspect child abuse, how to make a discipline referral to the assistant principal, and how to complete insurance and W-2 forms. Orientation is all about information—so much information that the overwhelmed novice can scarcely process it all.

In many districts, however, induction lasts well beyond the initial orientation. It is considered to be the time period in which "newly authorized professionals begin to establish their practice—in teaching, usually, the two years following employment as a teacher" (California Commission on Teacher Credentialing, 1998, p. 36). A variety of activities can and should take place during this induction period. Mager (1992) describes these as "an effort to assist new teachers in performing—that is, expressing their competence in the particular context to which they have been assigned—toward the end of being effective" (p. 20). The Ferguson-

Florissant School District in suburban St. Louis, aims to improve the effectiveness of beginning teachers by the following three efforts:

1. Developing a thorough understanding of the district's vision and mission

2. Communicating the district/school culture to the beginning teachers

3. Introducing the beginning teachers to the district's support system (Tom Cornell, personal communication March, 2001)

As part of their induction program and as mandated by Missouri law (Missouri Excellence in Education Act 5 CRS 80-800.010), each beginning teacher must be provided with a professional development plan that addresses the teacher's first 2 years in the classroom. The purpose of the plan is to assist, not to evaluate. In addition, the induction program provides for a mentor—"a coach, trainer, positive role model, developer of talent, and opener of doors."

> Mentoring is a process that facilitates instructional improvement wherein an experienced educator works with a novice or less experienced teacher collaboratively and nonjudgmentally to study and deliberate on ways instruction in the classroom may be improved. (Sullivan & Glanz, 2000, p. 128)

There are three kinds of mentoring:

1. A formal district program in which mentors are paid, given time off, and specific activities are expected and built in

2. An informal mentoring by grade-level teammates

3. The kind of informal mentoring or coaching a principal does in addition to the usual supervision responsibilities

The Principal's Role in the Mentoring Program

As a principal, you are no doubt working in one of the following three kinds of districts:

1. A district that has a well-established and highly successful induction program that includes a beginning of the year orientation, a mentoring program, and a comprehensive new teacher evaluation system

2. A district in which you are not only the principal, but also the supervisor, mentor, coach, and director of staff development

3. A district that is somewhere in between

If you work in the first kind of district, your mentoring program is in the very capable hands of one or more central-office administrators, a well-run faculty professional development committee, and a team of highly trained and supervised teacher-mentors. If you work in the second kind of district, you don't have the money, the time, or the energy to develop a formal mentoring program. If you work in the third kind of district, perhaps there are plans afoot to establish a more comprehensive program to support newcomers.

Whatever the size or sophistication of your school district, however, you are still the principal. When central office retreats to the administration center to collapse after their 3 days of orienting new teachers, you are in charge. When the mentors go off to their classrooms to assume their own not-insignificant teaching responsibilities, you have the job of helping new teachers survive. When the day of reckoning arrives in the spring—the time to make the decision regarding whether to retain or to dismiss—you are responsible for making it.

There are many ways that you as a principal can provide the help beginning teachers need without acting in the traditional mentor role. Principals cannot, in the strictest sense of the word, serve as mentors, since a mentor cannot be responsible for, nor be involved in the evaluative process. The principal who attempts to juggle both evaluation and mentoring will confuse the beginning teacher and frustrate the purposes of both processes. However, there are many things that you as a principal can do for new teachers to help them feel included, be successful, and want to come back for a second year. You may wonder when you'll find time to do any more than you are already doing. Adopt another perspective. The time you spend nurturing new teachers in the fall and winter months is time you won't have to spend in the spring—advertising, screening, interviewing, and orienting another crop of new teachers. The time you spend right now is time you won't have to spend later—"picking up the pieces" when a new teacher falls apart at the seams or falls under the spell of a negative staff member. Here are 30+ things that principals can do with and for new teachers to make them feel included and help them be successful. Some of the things will be done directly with and for beginning teachers; others are activities in which you will work behind the scenes and through staff members. Even if you have a well-established mentoring program in place, don't overlook the importance of team building and assimilation activities that bring experienced and beginning teachers together.

31 Things That Principals Can Do for and With New Teachers to Make Them Feel Included and Help Them Be Successful

1. *An Induction Ceremony.* Becoming a teacher should be marked with a ritual of passage (Gehrke, 1991). Patricia Phelps (1993) suggests that administrators consider a formal ceremony to celebrate the induction of new teachers into the profession. The ceremony might be held as a prelude to a new-teacher inservice, at the first meeting of new teachers and their mentors, or on the opening day of school when the entire staff gathers together for the first time in the new school year. Phelps further suggests a creed or pledge that new teachers might recite to include statements like "I will share my experiences in the classroom with other educators in a positive manner," or "I will express my appreciation to students, administrators, and peers for the successes I have" (Phelps, 1993, p. 154). Veteran teachers would then respond to the new teachers' pledge with one of their own. For example, "we shall support, encourage, and listen to these new teachers and share with them our knowledge, empathetic understanding, and positive advice" (1993, p. 154). Put the planning in the hands of three or four teachers who appreciate the importance of tradition and ceremony. Done right, this activity can be a winner.

2. *A Picture Is Worth a Thousand Words.* Don't just tell new teachers what you expect of them on the first day of school; show them. The first day of school lays the foundation for the rest of the school year. Show your newcomers a video titled *The First Day of School*, produced and directed by a talented parent, staff member, or both. Open with shots of students—waiting with their parents out on the playground, arriving by

bus, or, if yours is a high school campus, out in the parking lot driving up in their own cars. Record portions of an opening assembly if you have one. Finally, include footage of various teachers explaining rules, routines, and procedures to their students. Show the tape during your building orientation for new teachers, make copies available for new teachers to check out and view on their own, or both.

3. *Behind the Scenes.* Introduce each new teacher to the custodial, secretarial, attendance, and health staff. Explain to new teachers the importance of these folks to the smooth running of the school and suggest that they take time to learn their names, chat with them briefly as appropriate, and from time to time throughout the year, show their appreciation for the contributions they make to the academic program of the school.

4. *Making a List and Checking It Twice.* Develop a checklist of opening day activities in the classroom and hold new teachers accountable for completing it prior to your first meeting together (Brooks, 1985). The Oxnard Union High School District includes an accountability checklist inside its orientation packet. On the left side of the page are questions and on the right side of the page are spaces for teachers to write in their answers. Teachers are asked: "What is your policy regarding: (a) heading papers, (b) use of pen or pencil, (c) writing on back of paper, (d) neatness, (e) incomplete work, (f) late work, (g) missing work, (h) due dates, and (i) makeup work?" Another question asks: "How do you intend to (a) post assignments, (b) let students know assignments were missed while they were absent, (c) explain how assignments will be graded, (d) keep students aware of requirements for long-term assignments?" (Oxnard Union High School District, 2000; Mike Smith, personal communication, March 2001). This checklist ensures that new teachers will have thought through those all-important first-day issues well in advance of the first day.

5. *Celebration!* Celebrate your school. When new staff members are formally introduced in your first faculty meeting, take time to celebrate the uniqueness of your school. Ask each returning staff member to write down one thing that they especially like about working at ABC school. Ask the new teachers to write down why they are looking forward to working at ABC school. When everyone is finished, divide into groups of

five to eight and share. Then, ask a reporter in each group to summarize the feelings of his or her group.

6. *The New Teachers' Lending Library.* Assemble a set of books that new teachers will find especially helpful. Locate multiple copies of titles like *Teaching Gifted Kids in the Regular Classroom* (Winebrenner, 1992); *Teaching Kids With Learning Difficulties in the Regular Classroom* (Winebrenner, 1996); *How to Be an Effective Teacher: The First Days of School* (Wong & Wong, 1998); and *Discipline Strategies for the Bored, Belligerent, and Ballistic in Your Classroom* (Fuery, 1994) in the media center where new teachers can check them out.

7. *Have Job, Will Travel.* Remember that many new staff members will be itinerant. Unfortunately they won't all be in your building together on any given day, so you may need to repeat some of your orientation activities several times. Give them a special welcome to your school. These "wandering teachers" are eager to feel a part of a school, any school, but are often overlooked. Along with a warm greeting, give them the ground rules in your building—where they should report or sign in when they arrive at the building, what they should do if they are unavoidably detained by an emergency, and who to call in the event of an absence. Extend a personal invitation to each one to attend the next faculty meeting. Make a point of introducing them publicly to everyone. Itinerant staff members need the cooperation and support of all of their colleagues to do their jobs well, but they often have limited access to people because of their schedules. Do all you can to help them become part of the staff—invite them to social events; include them in planning buildingwide events; and keep them informed of news of students and families with whom they may work.

8. *Think Ahead.* Ask your secretary to order extra staplers, staples, scissors, scotch tape dispensers, red pens, plan books, and grade books. These items have a way of walking off from vacant classrooms over the summer, and there's nothing more discouraging to a new teacher than to be told, "You'll have to fill out a requisition."

9. *Make It Your Own!* Reserve money in the budget for every new teacher to buy some supplies and materials of their own choosing. Sandra Ahola gives each new teacher some order forms, suggests that they check out their classroom to see what it contains, and then submit

an order for those special things they might need to make the classroom their own.

10. *A Visible Presence.* Be a visible presence in the classrooms of new teachers during the early weeks of the school year. "I pop in and out of classes like a 'jack-in-the-box' in the beginning," says Sandra Ahola. "I try very hard not to intimidate new teachers or put them under pressure, but I want them to know that I am available and interested in how they are doing."

11. *Say Something Nice.* Intentionally offer a brief word or two of praise to each new staff member during the first week of school. Do you remember the last time you were a newcomer? You kept wondering how you were doing. You felt a little anxious and craved reassurance. Make the praise specific to something the teacher has done well. Compliments about appearance or accomplishments outside of school don't count. "To be effective with teachers, it seems, praise must be connected to professional accomplishments" (Blase & Kirby, 2000, p. 17).

12. *Smile. You're on Candid Camera.* Smile and speak to new teachers regularly. Actually, I recommend smiling and speaking to every teacher every day, but I am realistic enough to know that the first days of school are hectic. However, please don't look frantic, distracted, annoyed, or irritated when you pass a new teacher in the hallway or pop into a classroom for a quick visit. That teacher will automatically assume that your demeanor is a direct result of something he or she did and will worry about it for days.

13. *Reach Out and Touch Someone.* Meet with new teachers once a week during the first semester. Don't rely solely on the mentors you have assigned to handle every question a new teacher may have. Meet regularly with your new teachers to focus on philosophical issues, parental problems, or grading. Choose a different topic for each meeting. Serve refreshments and keep the conversation flowing. Don't lecture. Listen. "New teachers can sometimes get off on the wrong foot and not even realize what they're doing," advises Sandra Ahola. "It's up to the principal to catch problems before they get big."

14. *The New Teacher's Survival Guide.* Develop a short, easy-to-read guide specific to your building. Jan Antrim puts together a condensed,

nuts-and-bolts version of the handbook containing all of the information her new teachers need to make it through the first week—schedules, substitutes, drills, telephone numbers, and so forth.

15. *Share the Vision.* Share your school's mission statement and school-improvement plan with new staff members. Provide copies and talk with them about what it really means. Describe the process used to write the mission so that new teachers will know the story behind it. Also, talk about the school-improvement plan, how it was developed, what the new teachers' roles will be in meeting the goals, and whom they can consult for help in implementing specific aspects of the plan. Take a few minutes to talk about your personal vision for the school. Let new staff members feel your energy and passion. Let them know that you consider them to be an important part of realizing that vision.

16. *An Observation Is Worth a Thousand Words.* Provide opportunities for in-house observations. Kathy Miller schedules from one to three opportunities for new teachers to observe master teachers at work during the first semester. Kathy and the teacher jointly decide what should be the focus during the observation—behavioral strategies, teaching techniques, or perhaps an aspect of curriculum.

17. *The New Teacher's Survival Kit.* Give every new teacher his or her own personal survival kit. Package one or two helpful books (depending on your budget) in a basket with a district coffee mug, several small packages of cookies or crackers for those after-school "snack attacks," a bottle of Excedrin, and two free passes to leave school early. Include books like *Winning Year One: A Survival Manual for First-Year Teachers* (Fuery, 1989); *How to Be an Effective Teacher: The First Days of School* (Wong & Wong, 1998); *You Have to Go to School—You're the Teacher* (Rosenblum-Lowden, 2000); or *My First Year as a Teacher* (Kane, 1991).

18. *The Black Binder.* When I was an elementary principal, I published a bulletin every Monday morning. It was printed on three-hole paper so faculty members could slip it into a binder and have it readily accessible. These bulletins contained information that was available nowhere else: the dates, times, and participants of all of the meetings scheduled to be held during the coming week (e.g., staffings, informational meetings, parent conferences, district curriculum meetings); announcements of any special events in the building (e.g., assemblies, visitors to

classrooms); notices of any faculty social events; substitutes scheduled into the building for staff development days; plus anything else that was important for teachers to know. I also let teachers know when I would be out of the building for administrative meetings, staffings, or workshops. The most important part of the bulletin (in my opinion, of course) was my weekly message—words of praise and encouragement to teachers for accomplishments during the past week, and some inspiration or a touch of humor to fire up their engines on Monday morning. Sometimes I attached an article that I thought would be helpful. Staff members quickly learned how valuable this document was and saved back issues as a ready reference. The teachers who failed to read the bulletin, even for a week, soon found themselves out of the information loop, for we never discussed administrivia at faculty meetings. We used those precious minutes for instructional and curricular issues. I gave copies of the last three issues of the weekly bulletin to new teachers so they could gain a sense of its importance in the organizational life of our school. I reinforced for them the importance of reading it carefully each week, highlighting the events and meetings and information that were applicable to them, and then putting that information into their plan book or daily planner. I gave each new teacher a brand-new black binder in which to store his or her faculty bulletins.

19. *The Secretary's Orientation.* Ask your secretary to give new teachers a brief orientation of the office. This activity will not only boost your secretary's morale, but save you valuable time and help new teachers bond with the secretary. Topics to cover might include the following: how to operate the photocopy machine, mail box procedures, how to schedule field trips, how to obtain needed supplies, how to fill out requisitions, and how to use the phone system to forward calls and make personal phone calls. If you don't schedule this kind of orientation, the secretary will be constantly interrupted to explain the intricacies of the photocopier to each new teacher.

20. *Honesty Is the Best Policy.* Be honest with new teachers. Every principal has a few pet peeves that new teachers should know about up front. Personally, I hated surprises and shared my distaste for being blindsided the first time I met with new teachers. I told them that if they were having a problem, either with a specific student or a parent, I wanted to know about it right away so I could be informed and make them look good. Another one of my pet peeves was tardiness. I told new

teachers that I understood there would be emergencies and unexpected crises, but that I expected them to be on time otherwise. A pattern of tardiness always made me cranky, I told them, and they certainly didn't want a cranky principal. If there's some kind of unwritten dress code, let teachers know what it is immediately. One other important message I shared with new staff was the value I placed on teachers being respectful to one another, respectful to their students and parents, and respectful to support personnel like secretaries, custodians, lunchroom supervisors, and bus drivers. I told them I didn't care about their wonderful lesson plans, if they weren't nice people. Don't make new teachers guess what they need to do to make you a happy principal. Spell it out on the first day.

21. *The Dreaded Evaluation!* Explain the evaluation process to new teachers personally and face-to-face. The district office will do an inservice on the contract and the evaluation process. The union will do an inservice on the contract and the evaluation process. However, you should do one of your own. You will be the person doing the evaluating. Let them hear what will happen from your perspective. Schedule a general meeting for all new teachers in your building to go over the formal evaluation process step-by-step. New teachers are terrified of evaluation. They have not only heard horror stories in their preservice training, but your staff has no doubt already updated them on how many new teachers you didn't invite back after their first year. Explain the purpose of evaluation, all of the ins and outs of the instrument and what the language means. Pay special attention to the timelines so that new teachers will know what to expect. I told them that by the time the first formal evaluation rolled around I would have been in their classroom so many times, their initial nervousness would have worn off. Their students would be used to seeing me and so would they. I also promised that if I had a question or concern about something, I would tell them about it immediately so they could do something about it.

22. *Halloween and Homecoming.* These are major events in the calendars of schools. In advance of these events or others, take time to brief new teachers about the past practices, problems, and your personal preferences regarding their participation. Often the contract specifies who supervises what and when, but given a choice you'll want new teachers to get involved and they will want to be.

23. *An Up-Front Investment.* Save some staff-development dollars to invest in brand-new teachers. If they are struggling with some aspect of classroom life, give them a morning off to meet with a mentor, grade-level team teacher, or central-office curriculum specialist to talk about the problem and structure a possible solution. Principals can provide this kind of coaching, but new teachers will feel more relaxed knowing that the person who will evaluate them isn't the one helping them out of a teaching dilemma.

24. *Role-Playing.* Recruit several of your more experienced and dramatic teachers to do some role-playing involving parent-teacher conferences. Give new teachers pointers on how to conduct a positive parent-teacher conference, deal with angry or hostile parents, and what to do when they feel threatened or frightened (McEwan, 1998a).

25. *Curriculum Nights and Open Houses.* Produce a videotape of one or more of your most effective teachers conducting a curriculum night or open-house meeting with parents. Give new teachers the sense of what "a good one" looks like. View the tape along with new teachers and answer any questions they may have.

26. *The School Culture.* Build a culture in which teachers reach out to one another, work together, and consistently affirm one another. Some veteran teachers may have the attitude that "I survived; so can you" (Brock, 1990, p. 55). This rite-of-passage or trial-by-fire mentality can serve to isolate new teachers and cause them to feel discouraged. Unless the principal consistently articulates the responsibilities of the faculty to support and encourage new teachers and to make them feel a part of the staff, the likelihood of losing good teachers increases. A schoolwide willingness to support not only new teachers, but also every other colleague, only happens when it is modeled and expected by the instructional leader. Sharon Huffman's teachers know that she values flexibility, teamwork, collegiality, and solid collaboration. "They know," she says, "what we are about here, what the expectations for excellence are, and the priority I place on their care for children and their academic growth."

27. *Pass on the Vision.* Communicate the culture of your school to new teachers. Tell stories, show off trophies, look at scrapbooks, and celebrate heroes. The culture of a school is invisible, but principals and teachers can make it come alive for new teachers through storytelling

and the sharing of artifacts and documents. Routine behaviors, norms, and dominant values must be shared with newcomers if they are to "do and say the right things" that will make them feel a part of the faculty. Where to park, where to sit at lunchtime, and who collects money to send flowers when they are needed are amazingly important routines in the life of a school. Give newcomers the "scoop."

28. *Have a Little Fun.* Just before parent-teacher conferences, invite the new teacher(s) out for pizza and some fun. If you have too few new teachers for a party, invite their mentors or other congenial teachers to also attend. Begin around 4:30 p.m., meet at a local pizza parlor, order a round of soft drinks (no alcohol allowed), and just talk. Begin with an icebreaker question: "If your first few months of teaching at ABC School were a movie, what would the title be and who would have the starring role?" Possible answers might include *Mission Impossible, Survivor, Stand and Deliver, Animal House,* and so forth. The goal is to generate some laughter and fun, to relieve some of the anxiety and stress, and to gather renewed energy for the weeks until the holiday break.

29. *Teach the Teachers.* Organize support seminars and skills training for new teachers. Support seminars are monthly meetings that will be held ideally during release time, but more often than not are held after school. In some districts, central-office staff will plan these seminars, but if you work in a small district or in a one-school district, you are probably on your own. In the Richmond School District (British Columbia, Canada), the monthly seminar topics for new teachers include "Communicating: Parents, Colleagues and Students"; Planning: Beginning With the End in Mind"; "Stress and Time Management: One Term Down, Two to Go"; and "Supporting Diverse Learners: Success for All" (Linda Mackenzie, personal communication, February 12, 2001).

30. *Teachers Teaching Teachers.* Offer a stipend to an experienced teacher to present a session to newcomers on a specific topic. Extend an invitation to other staff members to attend as well, but design the seminar with the new teacher in mind.

31. *What's in a Name?* Be sure to order name plates or signs for the classroom doors as soon as you have hired new teachers. Check the spelling of each name carefully and remember to ask if there are any name changes on the horizon. When the building opens for business in

August, ask the custodian to install the name plates and ask the secretary to put up the names of new teachers on their mailboxes. New teachers always arrive early to work in their classrooms and there's nothing quite as exciting as seeing your name on your door as well as on the mailbox. By contrast, there's nothing quite as discouraging as retrieving one's mail from "someone else's mailbox" or teaching in a classroom with someone else's name on the door. It's the little things that count.

Teachers Teaching Teachers: Some Ways to Encourage Your Staff to Support New Teachers

The following set of activities is designed to encourage and enlist your experienced teachers to mentor and help new teachers. I use *encourage*, because if a mentoring program has not been institutionalized, money has not been budgeted, and roles have not been clearly defined, a principal can only encourage the teachers to mentor other teachers. To mentor anyone, but especially a beginning teacher, is a very demanding job, particularly if that individual is having any difficulties with parents, students, or with his or her administrator. One becomes emotionally attached to one's protégé or mentee. One becomes highly invested in the success of the mentee. Moreover, unless boundaries are carefully observed, one can become overly involved in a mentee's life. In addition to the time demands that often far exceed the allocated or budgeted time, there is the added stress and tension of being involved in the teaching life of another person. Administrators are no strangers to this kind of stress, but it is often surprising and even immobilizing to a fellow teacher. That is why the best mentoring programs are well administered, clearly defined, closely monitored, and adequately funded. You cannot run a mentoring program on a shoestring. Having said that, however, I offer the following suggestions for establishing a collegial culture in your building that supports teachers helping teachers—even if they're not getting paid to do so. Remember that all staff members will benefit from the following activities.

1. *Grade-Level Team Building.* Encourage and expect team building at grade levels. Provide release time in which grade-level teams can solve curricular problems, discuss instructional issues, and plan jointly for units, projects, or special events. In a collegial and collaborative environ-

ment, the beginning teacher will have the benefit of support from fellow team members.

2. *Learn for a Day.* Send a new teacher and an experienced one off together for a day to the same workshop. I know that my former superintendent would frown on this use of funds. His idea of being frugal was to send one person and have him or her summarize the day for everyone else. He just didn't understand that a 20-minute recap of a daylong workshop wasn't particularly inspiring or even helpful. Pick a buddy teacher who is noted for practical assistance, a strong shoulder to cry on, patience, understanding, and lots of positive reinforcement. The experienced teacher need not necessarily be a veteran. In fact, a teacher with 2 to 3 years of experience who is solidly in command of his or her classroom might be more beneficial in terms of support for a new teacher. I would caution against sending a male and female teacher off to a workshop together for obvious reasons.

3. *Ask a Veteran.* Ask an experienced teacher if he or she would be willing to work with a new teacher for a day (i.e., if you furnished a substitute for his or her classroom and threw in a couple of other perks to be named). The veteran teacher would then spend a half-day in the classroom of the beginning teacher to work with and observe the teacher. Then the two would spend the second half of the day in conversation and planning in the light of what had been observed. The experienced teacher will work twice as hard as usual—planning for a substitute, as well as spending a cognitively demanding day. The right teacher will jump at the chance, however, especially if this individual is interested in becoming a principal one day.

4. *Reflective Observation.* Arrange for a new teacher to observe a more experienced, but still relatively new teacher. Ask the new teacher to choose a particular focus for the observation (i.e., an aspect of curriculum, classroom management, student assessment, or lesson planning). Then identify the appropriate teacher to be visited and share the new teacher's focus. Following the observation, ask the new teacher to write a brief reflective paper that might include answers to the following questions:

1. What did you see during your observation that surprised you?

2. What did you see that you would like to try in your own classroom?
3. What did you see that raised questions in you mind?
4. What specific differences did you observe between your teaching and that of the teacher you observed?

5. *Team-Building Exercises.* During the first month of school, take time in a faculty meeting or early-release day to engage in team-building exercises. Whenever new members are added to your faculty team, the dynamics will change. When experienced staff members retire, newcomers and younger faculty will have to assume leadership roles. If you do not take the time to rebuild your team each year, you will soon discover it is no longer a team, but a group of individuals. Take your faculty through a team-building exercise to help them identify the roles they are well suited to playing (McEwan, 1997). Another way to help staff members appreciate one another's approaches to problem solving and communicating is to introduce them to the concept of Edward DeBono's six thinking hats (1999). I frequently use DeBono's approach in workshops and find that teachers relate to it very well. Once you have read DeBono's book, buy six hats in the colors he recommends (red, yellow, green, black, white, and blue). Pick out styles that go along with the thinking-communicating personalities described by DeBono. Introduce your teachers to the hats and the thinking styles and before the session is over, you will have given them a unique way to think about communicating and solving problems. You will find them talking about "having my red hat on" or "thinking with my black hat" to describe their approach or frame of mind in a discussion or problem-solving session.

6. *The Collaborative Approach.* "Collaboration is working together for a common end" (Fishbaugh, 1997, p. 4). Don't assume that successful staff development always means inviting a speaker in to talk to your teachers. Provide time for teachers to work together to solve problems, articulate curriculum, or agree on outcomes. Many principals talk about collaboration, but they expect teachers to do it on their own time. Give teachers time to collaborate on improvement plans for individuals or small groups of students. Give teachers time to collaborate on interdisciplinary units. Provide time for teachers to talk about what they believe is most important for students to be able to know and do when they leave your school.

7. *Too Much to Do, Too Little Time.* Many mentoring programs include a seminar on time management and stress for new teachers as if these topics were unique to newcomers. The problems of stress and time management are always with us. Plan a round-table sharing session or a short seminar for all teachers that addresses these issues.

8. *Share Your Favorite Instructional Strategy.* Before your next faculty meeting, ask each experienced teacher to arrive with a favorite teaching tip or strategy written on a sticky note or 3 × 5 card. Get the meeting started on time, organize into small groups with only one new teacher per small group, and ask the experienced teachers to quickly share their strategies with their group. Collect all of the strategies (ask people to include their names in case someone wants more information) and ask your secretary to put together a list of "Hot Teaching Tips" to be sent out with the faculty bulletin. Other variations of this activity might include sharing a classroom management strategy; tips for keeping cool when confronted with angry parents; or some time-tested advice for a brand-new teacher.

Recapping Chapter 8

Moving from one side of the desk (as a student) to the other side (as a teacher) is a shock to most brand-new teachers. They are no longer passengers; they are now in the driver's seat. Suddenly, they need to change a flat tire, read the road map, and be responsible for "getting there." The things you do as an instructional leader are critical to helping new teachers succeed. Administrators can no longer afford to take "the survival of the fittest" approach to inducting new teachers. We must be intentional and thoughtful about making them feel included and helping them move from first-year to first-rate (Brock & Grady, 1997).

Looking Ahead

New teachers aren't the only ones who need encouragement. Veteran teachers experience their own versions of stress, burnout, emotional exhaustion, depression, and depersonalization. They are in desperate need of revitalization. Experienced teachers need to be energized from time to time to remain highly effective teachers. The good news is that many of the techniques and activities you used with new teachers also work with their more experienced counterparts. Chapter 9, however, gives you dozens of ideas you can use to empower and energize experienced teachers.

Energizing and Empowering Experienced Teachers

All of the talk of reforming schooling must never lose sight of the ultimate goal: to create institutions where students can learn through interaction with teachers who are themselves always learning. The effective school must become an educative setting for its teachers if it aspires to become an educational environment for its students.

Shulman (1989, p. 186)

During any given school year your staff members will fall into roughly six categories or be situated at six points along a continuum in their educational practice:

1. Developing survival skills

2. Becoming competent in the basic skills of instruction

3. Expanding their instructional flexibility

4. Acquiring instructional expertise

5. Contributing to the growth of colleagues' instructional expertise

6. Participating in a broad array of educational decisions at all levels of the educational system (Leithwood, 1990, pp. 74-75)

Knowing which staff members are where on that continuum is essential to planning which activities and experiences to offer your teachers. Typical staff-development opportunities are often planned to meet the needs of administrators—implement a new curriculum, learn about a mandated program, comply with state regulations, or learn how to do something different so we can get better test scores. Sometimes, valuable time allocated for inservice is even regrettably wasted on administrivia.

Rarely are staff-development programs (districtwide committees and faculty input to the contrary) based on the real needs of teachers, presented by teacher-leaders, or both. I offer that observation as a former central-office administrator who was in charge of staff development for my district. I found the job quite frustrating and very humbling because there was so much I had to do and not enough time to do what I wanted to do or needed to do. Now that I'm on the other side of staff development—hired by multidistrict cooperatives, school districts, and individual schools to provide daylong workshops on a variety of topics related to school improvement—I experience a different set of frustrations. As carefully as I try to plan for the diverse nature of my audiences, I am always astounded by the folks who just happen to show up because they didn't have anywhere else to go. My last audience was made up of teachers (new and experienced from every level), principals (new and experienced from every level), a school nurse, a high school basketball coach, an audiology coordinator, and a truant officer.

Figuring out how best to empower and energize experienced teachers is one of the more challenging assignments you have.

Principals who empower their staffs do not simply turn teachers loose, let them go off and do whatever they want, and hope for the best. Instead they use core values and the intended curricular outcomes of the school to provide a clear structure which enables teachers to work within established boundaries in creative and autonomous ways. These principals demand rigid adherence to the values at the same time that they encourage innovation and autonomy in day-to-day operations. (DuFour, 1991, p. 34)

Exactly what is empowerment? It means that teachers will have a sense of shared ownership and responsibility, as well as a feeling of being in control of their destiny and direction. When teachers are empowered, they are confident, outgoing, and responsive. They are highly effective teachers. Experienced teachers will readily confess, however, that being the kind of teachers they want to be and know they can be—highly effective teachers—is difficult, if not impossible, when working in an unsupportive environment.

Empowerment begins with the belief that all people are capable of taking action to improve their work. The process gets underway when leaders express faith that others can and will meet high expectations. Instead of controlling people, leaders assist people in strengthening skills and developing their best attributes. This affirmation of competence elevates the spirit and status of everyone in the organization. People are more involved in their work as they are included in the decisions that affect their responsibility. (Bellon, 1988, pp. 30-31)

Teachers feel empowered when they have decision-making roles, experience professional growth through continued learning and collaboration, enjoy status in their schools, have a certain degree of autonomy, can see the impact of their influence and participation, and are efficacious (Short & Rinehart, 1992).

Following are 26 activities, strategies, and behaviors that principals can implement in their schools to empower and energize experienced teachers. These suggestions are drawn from my own personal experiences as a principal, suggestions from outstanding instructional leaders, and a variety of experts in the field of professional development.

26 Things That Principals Can Do to Empower and Energize Experienced Teachers

[A] good teacher renewal philosophy should help a teacher resolve his or her day-to-day problems through practical solutions that are both emotionally satisfying and aesthetically pleasing to the individual. In sum, we think a good teacher renewal philosophy ought to be rational,

true, morally justifiable, emotionally satisfying, and aesthetically pleasing.

Shea (1992, p. 13)

1. *Learning Circles.* "Learning circles are small communities of learners among teachers . . . who come together intentionally for the purpose of supporting each other in the process of learning" (Collay, Dunlap, Enloe, & Gagnon, 1998). Learning circles can be short-term or long-lived, but they must become healthy communities of learners to differentiate themselves from externally driven district workshops, inservice sessions, or reform efforts. Learning circles can focus on a book (see the list of recommended readings for each of the 10 traits in Resource D); on a topic (see the list of reflective questions and topics in Resource E); on a content area; or on the learning process itself.

2. *Walking Your Talk.* Sally Roth models energy, positive power, and love. "I do this," she explains, "by trying to care for each person, to look for what they do well and reinforce it." Here are just some of the ways that Sally energizes her teachers:

- She praises them privately (letters, notes, talks, evaluations, and candy kisses, etc.).
- She arranges for them to have time for planning collaboratively with each other.
- She says yes to as many of their ideas as she possibly can and when she has to say no she gives a rationale that can be understood.
- She understands when teachers are ill.
- She understands when teachers' children are ill.
- She encourages her teachers to change rooms, grade levels, or teaching assignments.
- She goes out on a limb and takes her teachers out there with her.
- When teachers are about to burn out, she gives them hugs and lets them cry if they need to.
- She fights for lower class sizes whenever she can.
- She spares teachers unnecessary trivia and paperwork whenever possible.
- She shows them hard data whenever possible to verify that they are succeeding with kids.

- She supports teachers in front of parents (and counsels or reprimands them in private).
- She buys the best materials for her teachers that the budget will permit.
- She updates them often about what is going on in the school.

3. *Play to the Strengths of Your Team.* Sandra Ahola believes in spending 90% of her time with 90% of her staff—"feeding the leaders," as she puts it. "I find each person's area of strength and build on it." Do you know what your strengths are? Have you taken the time to think about the specific strengths of each of your staff members? Are you using those strengths (e.g., writing abilities, speaking abilities, coaching abilities, facilitative abilities) to empower and energize other teachers?

4. *Become a Champion Fund-Raiser.* Sandra Ahola is a champion fund-raiser. "I find that if you unleash leaders in your school and reward them well, they will move the whole school." Sandra has learned how to tap into central-office grants to find money for release days, minigrants for innovative ideas, and stipends for teachers who present at staff meetings, Board of Education meetings, or conferences. I second Sandra's efforts to make money available. The Foundation for Educational Excellence in my district allocated thousands of dollars every year for teacher minigrants. I was always amazed and delighted at the intense creativity and extra effort that the promise of several hundred dollars elicited from teachers.

5. *Praise.* Blase and Kirby (2000) discovered that teachers viewed praise as a positive and effective influence strategy and that it increased their sense of belonging and motivation, and left them feeling encouraged. Sharon Huffman uses her bimonthly faculty meetings to share and celebrate teachers' achievements, a practice that Blase and Blase highly recommend. Sharon acknowledges that "my own best work with children is essentially through the success of my faculty. I give them credit for student learning progress." She targets her praise to teachers' work, a practice that Blase and Blase (1998) also found particularly meaningful to teachers.

6. *Focus on the Mission.* "Staff development will never have its intended effect as long as it is grafted on schools in the form of discrete, unconnected projects" (Fullan, 1990, p. 3). Make sure that every

professional-development activity you sponsor, promote, endorse, or institute has a connection to the mission of your school. A case can always be made for development that improves instruction, but sending teachers to workshops that are not specifically linked to the focus in your school can often have the unintended effect of taking teachers off-task.

7. *Leadership Teams.* When we first established a building leadership team at Lincoln School in the early 1980s, it was the first time that any of us, either principal or teachers, had ever participated in such an endeavor. However, our substandard achievement and low morale made us a perfect laboratory for experimenting with the power of shared decision making and responsibility. We spent one afternoon per month wrestling with problems of instruction, curriculum, staff development, and change. I'll never forget the experience. Each year two members rotated off and two new members joined the group. Before long, almost every experienced teacher had been a part of the group and had presented proposals to the faculty; taken responsibilities for decision making; changed their problem-solving paradigms; and experienced the positives as well as the pain that sometimes comes with leadership.

8. *Peer Coaching or Consultation.* Peer coaching involves teachers helping teachers—a practice that sounds quite lovely. However, any time a teacher invites another teacher into his or her classroom for the purposes of observing and offering feedback, there is bound to be a measure of reluctance or tension, at least in the beginning. Our building leadership team developed the peer-coaching program at Lincoln School, and they did a marvelous marketing job to convince several of our more senior teachers that they had everything to gain and nothing to lose from such a venture. Although all of our teachers had been trained in clinical supervision (i.e., a process of observation and conferencing), we used a modified version of the model developed by Goldsberry (1986) in which colleagues observed each other teaching and then attempted to identify patterns of teacher or learner behavior. Teachers were initially reluctant to engage in this activity, but we emphasized a data-based approach where the observer records information about either the teacher (e.g., how many positive versus negative comments were made; how many and what kind of attention-getting moves were used; or the differences in interactions with high-achieving vs. low-achieving students) or the students (what kind of on-task behavior is evidenced by the class as a whole). This approach removed the possibility of

subjective judgments that can be threatening to a teacher and focused on "just the facts." We spent much time in establishing ground rules that would maintain confidentiality and professionalism.

9. *Video Analysis.* Group viewing and analysis of a lesson is a powerful way to discover what teachers really think about instruction and engender lively discussion. I mentioned in the preface my experiences with groups of principals and teachers in viewing a commercially prepared videotape. However, if you have a particularly effective (and confident) teacher, tape a lesson, and then use it as the focus of discussion. I use just three questions:

- What behaviors of the teacher were effective and should be continued in further lessons?
- What behaviors of the teacher were ineffective and should be eliminated or minimized in further lessons?
- What effective teaching behaviors that were missing from the lesson should be initiated/included in subsequent lessons?

Other activities might include charting time-on-task behaviors or determining the ratio of positive reinforcing comments to negative critical comments.

10. *Situational Supervision.* Work with teachers to improve instruction using different strokes for different folks. New staff members will no doubt need a more directive informational approach, but experienced staff will feel more empowered if you collaborate with them or even let the teacher set the agenda. Pay attention to the continuum mentioned earlier to determine where teachers are and what they specifically need for continued growth.

11. *Structured Professional Dialogue.* If you are contemplating a change in practice or curriculum, structuring a professional dialogue is a good way to organize the debate and discussion about it. Anyone can lead the dialogue, but a teacher who has done some prior research, attended a workshop, or has done some experimentation in his or her classroom is the best candidate. The discussion takes place in three steps.

- Someone, usually the group leader, presents a summary of the views of the experts and the research findings.

- Then, group members analyze the information and share their own personal experiences and knowledge regarding the topic.
- Finally, the discussion turns to how what has been read and learned can inform practice in the classroom (Glatthorn, 1987).

This structured dialogue can be a self-contained process, or it could be held in the nature of a fish-bowl exercise in which a larger group of faculty members sit in a circle around the dialogue members and eavesdrop on the conversation.

12. *Feedback to the Principal.* Nothing empowers teachers more than to feel that their principal listens and heeds what they have to say. Kathy Miller asks her teachers for feedback regarding how well she supports them and the schools' goals for increasing student learning. I did the same thing. Each spring I asked the teachers (and other staff members as well) to answer three questions in the light of our school mission:

- What am I doing that you would like me to keep on doing?
- What am I doing that is ineffective and should be stopped?
- What am I not doing that you think I should start doing?

My building leadership team members collected and collated this feedback and then one of the team met with me to discuss and explain the results. Although the process always included a measure of discomfort as I realized how much I still had to learn about being a principal, there were also moments of intense satisfaction when I discovered how greatly what I did was appreciated.

13. *Model Good Teaching.* Yvonne Peck, assistant principal at Frontier High School, in Camarillo, California, recently moved into administration from the ranks of teaching and frequently uses her own teaching talents to model for new staff members. "I've given workshops on reading, brain-based learning, and classroom management." When she's giving advice and meeting one on one, Yvonne explains, any advice is filtered through the medium of evaluation. When she's teaching, staff members feel less threatened: "They can accept or reject what I say without the kind of defensive attitude that is sometimes engendered when I give unsolicited advice."

14. *Action Research.* Action research is a type of applied research in which educators engage in reflective activities about their work (Sullivan & Glanz, 2000). After framing a research question, the teacher will collect data (e.g., test scores, questionnaires, observations, etc.) and then analyze and interpret the data.

15. *Self-Analysis of Videotapes.* DuFour (1991) makes a point when he reminds us of the ways in which professional athletes review videotapes of their performances, looking for flaws in their technique. He goes on to suggest that teachers can benefit from videotaping their teaching and watching it privately at first and then with a peer. At the outset of our peer-coaching program, there were several teachers who were very reluctant to be observed by anyone other than the principal. We suggested the videotaping option as a transitional strategy and found that once teachers became comfortable with the tripod and camera in their classroom, they could more readily accept an observer.

16. *Train Your Own Staff Development Cadre.* I constantly encouraged my teachers to take their skills and ideas on the road and become a teacher of teachers. Joan Will was my reading teacher and I remember a discussion we had after a particularly dismal presentation by a staff developer from the county office. "I could do that," said Joan. "You not only could do that. You'd be much better," I agreed, and immediately signed her up to present at our next inservice day. Once she had spoken so boldly, she began to get cold feet, but I held her hand, walked her through the presentation, and cheered her on from the front row. Today, she's a star—presenting on strategic reading all over the county and directing the reading program in the district. When Adrienne Johnson came back to work after raising her family, she had some "new teacher" jitters that were understandable. When I asked her to be the gifted facilitator at the middle school, she turned me down flat. I was desperate and convinced her that she was perfect for the job. And she was. She just didn't recognize it at that point. Our job as administrators is to recognize talent and develop it. More than 10 years later, Adrienne is energized and empowered, an example of what can happen when teachers become teachers of teachers.

17. *Reflective Practice.* Kathy Miller encourages her teachers to routinely engage in self-reflection with regard to their teaching and their interactions with students and parents. If we want teachers to learn, they

must constantly reflect on their teaching. Collay et al. (1998) suggest that documenting one's reflections is a condition for creating a healthy community of learners.

The documentation becomes more than a simple record of accomplishment as it is also an additional way to construct new knowledge. Structured reflection requires learners to look back at goals set and met or not met, on serendipitous learning and questions that surprised them, and toward insights that may occur when their new learning shifts part or all of their original beliefs in teaching (Collay et al., 1998, p. 11).

Consider using some of the reflective questions found in Resource E. Choose one and use it as a journal-writing experience at your next faculty meeting. Then assemble in small groups to talk about what teachers have written.

18. *Writing for Publication.* I submitted an article for publication during my early years of classroom teaching and continued to write for journals during my years as a media specialist and principal. In 1987, I wrote my first book, and I haven't stopped writing since. Writing for publication empowers one in many of the ways mentioned earlier: gaining professional growth through continued learning and collaboration, enjoying status, and being able to see the impact of one's influence. You will recall that several of the highly effective teachers who contributed to this book regularly communicate their ideas, beliefs, and values about teaching and education, not only to their school communities, but also to a more public audience. Donna Garner (1997), Carol Jago (2000), Jerry Jesness (1998, 1999, 2000a, 2000b), and Linda Taylor (1995, 2001) are all published authors. They write columns, op-ed pieces, books, articles, and curricula. Your staff members may not write a book for their first project, but how about encouraging them to contribute a newsletter article, a weekly column for the local paper, or an article for a professional journal about a particularly successful unit or project.

19. *The Principal's Book Club for Teachers.* Offer to buy copies of a selected book for every staff member who joins your book club. Or enlist a teacher to lead the club. Suggest a book or two drawn from the recommended reading list in Resource D. There are titles for each of the 10 traits.

20. *Curriculum Development.* As an assistant superintendent for instruction, I spent a good share of my working hours with staff members

doing curriculum development. Glatthorn (1987) defines it as "a cooperative enterprise among teachers by which they modify the district curriculum guides" (p. 32). We didn't just write curriculum guides, however. In the area of mathematics, we developed lessons that deepened students' understanding of topics not covered in our textbook. We designed units for gifted students that provided activities, assignments, and lessons that extended the regular curriculum. We also developed our own district performance-based assessments in science, reading, and mathematics. Working on curriculum stretches the mind, sharpens the focus, and increases a teacher's effectiveness in the classroom.

21. *Journals.* The exercises to energize experienced educators found in Resource E would be perfect probes for a teacher who wants to try his or her hand at writing. Suggest this kind of exercise to a teacher who is particularly discouraged or thinking of leaving the profession, or put together a journal-writing group that meets once or twice a month to share some of their writings. Who knows? Someone in the group may just turn their journal into a book!

22. *The School as a Learning Community.* There are many different models of staff development, and I have tried just about all of them. The one I would implement today, if I were to become a principal again, is one in which the school strives to become a learning community, not only for its students, but for its teachers. The most important element that is missing in our current school structure is time. In other countries (e.g., Japan) teachers are given time to plan lessons collaboratively, teach them for each other, and then gather again to talk about, fine-tune, and improve them (Yoshida, 1999). In my school as a learning community, I would beg, borrow, and steal more time for teachers to work together. I heartily concur with Raywid (1993):

> If collaborative endeavor is necessary to school adequacy, then schools must provide it. The responsibility rests with schools not individual teachers. Further, administrators, policymakers, and public alike must accept a new conception of school time. If we are to redefine teachers' responsibilities to include collaborative sessions with colleagues—and both organizational research and teacher effectiveness research now suggest they are essential to good schools—then it is necessary to reconstrue teacher time. (p. 34)

23. *A Teacher's IEP: The IDP.* Often the same old evaluation instrument can stifle an experienced staff member's professional development. If you have the flexibility, consider the teacher's version of an IEP, the IDP (Individualized Development Plan). Guskey (2000) recommends that only those teachers who are capable of self-direction and self-initiated learning be encouraged to use an individually guided model. Activities like self-analysis, personal reflection, personal histories, journal writing, and portfolios can be considered for inclusion in the plan (Guskey, 2000).

24. *Team Teaching.* Joanna, one of my staff members, was petrified about implementing our new reading program (Cooperative Integrated Reading and Composition). It involved using cooperative learning groups, writing strategies, and disbanded the traditional reading groups that had been her mainstay for years. Furthermore, she was worried about one particular set of parents; their child was gifted and they were certain to complain about the heterogeneous grouping plan. "Why don't we teach together the first week?" I asked. "I haven't taught reading for years, but I went through the training just like you did. We can learn together." She was so unprepared for this offer that she didn't have a good reason to refuse. Besides, she reasoned, I could teach when the Johnsons came to observe the new program in action. Both Joanna and I grew professionally during that week together. I modeled risk taking, a few good instructional strategies I still had in my tool kit, and we both learned to trust each other far more than we had in the past. Joanna respected my willingness to roll up my sleeves and teach reading for a week, and I respected her willingness to let me be in her classroom every day. It marked the beginning of a new relationship between us.

25. *Study Groups.* Study groups differ from both learning circles and structured-dialogue groups. Learning circles typically focus on issues of concern and great interest to teachers, but do not necessarily involve another agenda, such as school improvement or curricular change. Structured-dialogue groups typically address issues that may be controversial in nature and need a tightly structured format. Study groups, by contrast, typically choose a topic or issue to research and study with a goal of making recommendations to the principal, the building leadership team, or to the faculty as a whole. For example, perhaps your school is reviewing its math curriculum and instruction. The TIMSS (Third International Mathematics and Science Study) raised many troubling

questions about the ways we teach math in the United States. As the principal, you would like to know what can be learned from studying how teachers in other countries and cultures approach math instruction. To prepare for the study group, you might gather a library of resource materials regarding the topic, emphasizing to your teachers that the purpose of the group is to explore and learn, both from the materials and from each other. Here are some of the materials you might make available to the study group:

- Lewis, C., & Tsuchida, I. (1998). A lesson is like a swiftly flowing river: How research lessons improve Japanese education. *American Educator, 22*(4), 12-17, 50-52.
- Shimahara, N. K. (1998). The Japanese model of professional development: Teaching as a craft. *Teaching and Teacher Education, 14,* 451-462.
- Stigler, J. W., & Hiebert, J. (1997, January). Understanding and improving classroom mathematics instruction: An overview of the TIMSS video study. *Phi Delta Kappan,* pp. 14-21.
- Stigler, J. W., & Hiebert, J. (1999). *The teaching gap.* New York: The Free Press.
- U.S. Department of Education. (1999). *Attaining Excellence: A TIMMS resource kit* (#065-000-01013-5). Pittsburgh, PA: U.S. Government Printing Office.

26. *Reflective Exercises to Energize and Motivate Experience Teachers.* Resource E contains a variety of reflective questions, writing probes, and exercises to energize experienced teachers. They can be used by individuals who wish to write reflectively in a journal or as group exercises in a learning circle. Some are more appropriate for small groups and others will work well with an entire faculty. If you need a little something to get your teachers thinking about teaching, you will find it here.

Recapping Chapter 9

Coaching is face-to-face leadership that pulls together people with diverse backgrounds, talents, and experiences, and interests; encourages them to step up to responsibility and continued achievement; and treats them as full-scale partners and contributors.

Peters & Austin (1985, p. 264)

Instructional leaders function as unique amalgams of ombuds-men, reference librarians, and genies-in-a-bottle as they constantly help faculty to find the solutions to frustrating and difficult instructional problems. Teachers cannot do it by themselves. Highly effective teachers need strong instructional leaders standing behind, beside, and when necessary, in front of them to encourage, empower, motivate, and energize.

Conclusion

There are two kinds of books—books that you forget about minutes after you've finished reading them and books that stir you up, cause you to think, and even move you to action. I'm not naïve enough to think that *Ten Traits of Highly Effective Teachers* is a life-changing book. However, I am hoping that because you've read it, you will feel compelled to do the following:

1. Think more deeply about teaching

2. Try at least some the ideas you've encountered

3. Have a deeper appreciation for the complexities and intricacies of teaching

What Will You, the Reader, Do With What You've Learned?

If you are a principal, I hope that you will more frequently and readily affirm the talents and status of the highly effective teachers in your school. I hope that you will look at teaching in a new way—in the context of the 10 traits. As you hire, coach, and work with teachers on a daily basis, consider the 10 traits as benchmarks. I also hope you will make sure that every teacher to whom you entrust students on a daily basis is the kind of teacher you would want for your own children or grandchildren. Every child deserves highly effective teachers. Think carefully about those you hire.

If you are a teacher, I hope you will feel a renewed sense of calling and appreciation for your vocation. I hope that you'll be motivated to reflect more, read more, and talk more about the art of teaching with fellow teachers and administrators. Teaching is too difficult to go it alone. I also hope that you will remind yourself from time to time that teaching is a challenging profession. It's not always you—sometimes it is teaching. You've read what our experts have observed. Teaching is lonely and isolated (Sarason, 1971), fraught with uncertainties and a shadowed social standing (Lortie, 1975), confused about its purpose (Lieberman & Miller, 1984), and characterized by mess and noise (Goodwin, 1987). If you want to solve problems in a relatively ill-structured, dynamic environment (van der Sijde, 1990) that is constantly changing (Highet, 1976) and has only recently emerged from the stages of "witch doctoring" (Hunter, 1984, p. 169), then sign right here on the dotted line. If you are a teacher, you must carefully tend to your mental life, as well as your emotional and physical health. Teaching is tough and can take its toll, even on the best and the brightest. Spend time with people who affirm and appreciate you.

If you hire teachers (i.e., are a central-office human resources administrator), get out there and teach once in a while. Leave your computer databases and carefully calibrated screening instruments—spend a day in classrooms with students and their dedicated teachers. Walk the hallways. Talk to the consumers of education and find out what they value in teachers. After you have listened and observed, be a teacher for a day. We all started in the classroom, but it's easy to forget how hard it is. It is one thing to ask candidates questions about teaching; it is quite another matter to do it.

If you train teachers, recruit the best and brightest. Screen your applicants and please be honest with them: "You're not suited to teaching. You're not metacognitive enough. You're not responsive enough. You're not positive and real. You just aren't with-it!" Listen to the educators in the trenches who daily feel the pressures of accountability. Send them teachers who can teach.

What Will I, the Author, Do With What I've Learned?

Every book I write, and I've written more than 30, changes me in some way. Just as the teacher gains a new depth of understanding from teaching a lesson for the first time, an author learns more deeply about a subject by writing a new book. *Ten Traits of Highly Effective Teachers* has engaged me in unusual ways. As I prepare for my workshops, I am now thinking about the 10 traits. As I talk with my daughter about planning an activity for her two sections of Anthropology 101, I'm looking at what she's doing through a new lens—a trifocal lens. I am seeing the personal traits, the teaching traits, and the knowledge traits. I'm seated on a new three-legged stool as I give my workshops—the presenter as a person, the presenter as a teacher, and the presenter as an expert. Those who attend want to see all three of those persons when they spend a day with me.

Writing this book has also given me a renewed appreciation for teachers—at all levels. The teachers I interviewed are no different than the hundreds of thousands of teachers that you know. If you randomly selected staff members in your school or district, you would find highly effective teachers just like the ones you met in this book—each one a unique amalgam of the personal traits that indicate character, the teaching traits that get results, and the intellectual traits that demonstrate knowledge, curiosity, and awareness.

What Are Your Goals?

I love to make lists. You have probably noticed that during your reading. I have made one for you, but I've only jotted down the numbers. You'll have to fill in the blanks. What are you going to do differently tomorrow? If you are inclined, send me a note (emcewan@mindspring. com) and tell me, or visit my Web site (www.elainemcewan.com) and contact me from there.

1.

2.

3.

4.

5.

Resource A

Graphic Organizers

Form 1.1. A Do-It-Yourself Ten Traits of Highly Effective Teachers

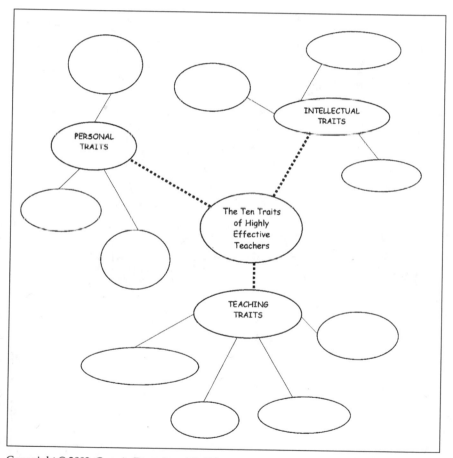

Figure 1.1. The Ten Traits of Highly Effective Teachers

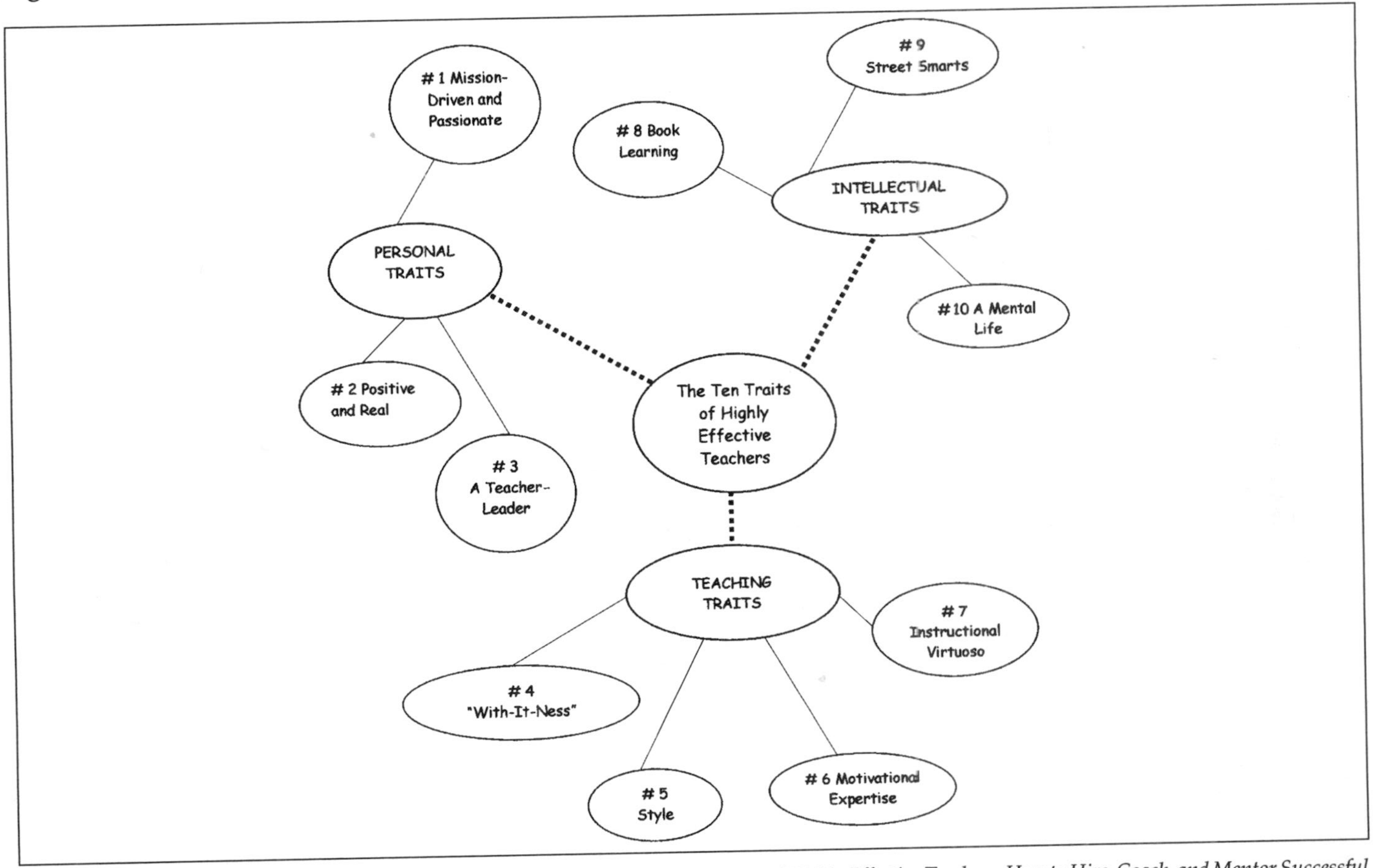

Figure 2.1. Personal Traits That Signify Character: What an Effective Teacher *Is*

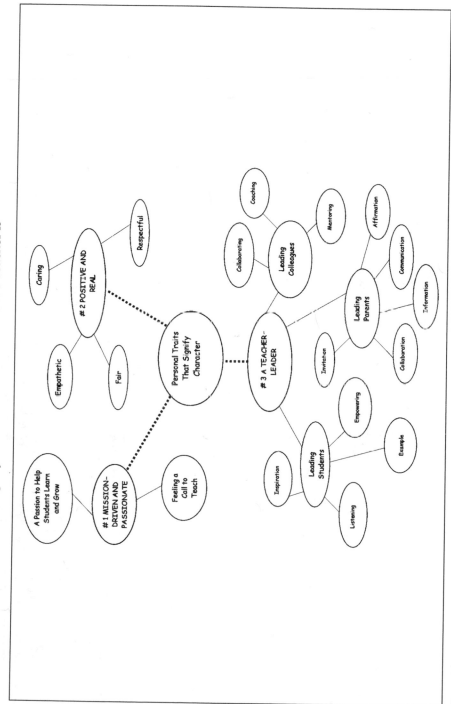

Figure 3.1. Trait 4: With-It-Ness

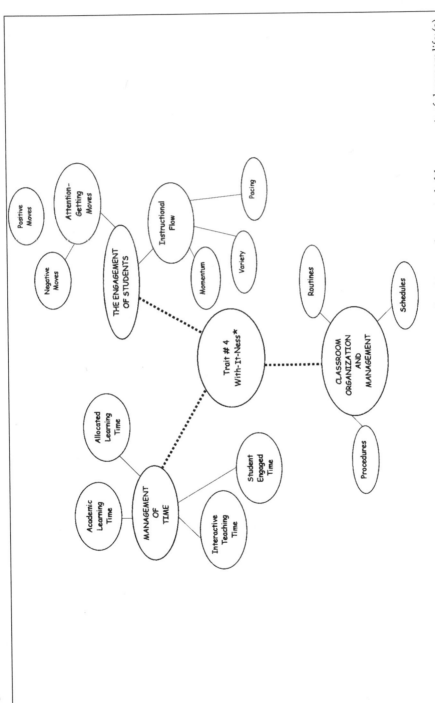

*"With-it-ness" is a state of being in which teachers are on top of, tuned in to, aware of, and in complete control of three aspects of classroom life: (a) organization and management, (b) the engagement of students, and 3) the management of time

Figure 3.2. Trait 5: Style

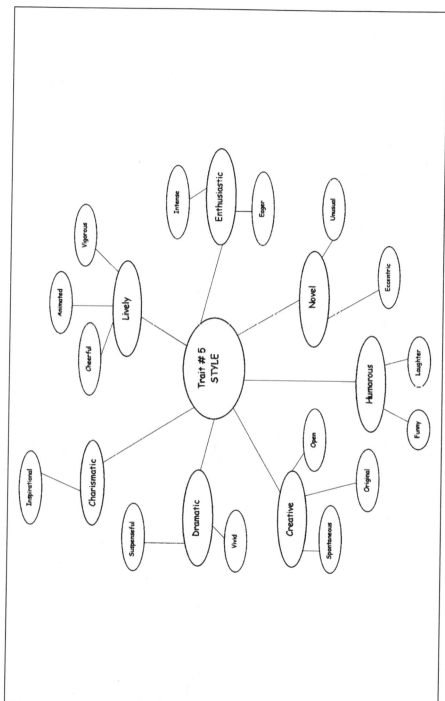

182

Figure 4.1 Trait 6: Motivational Expertise

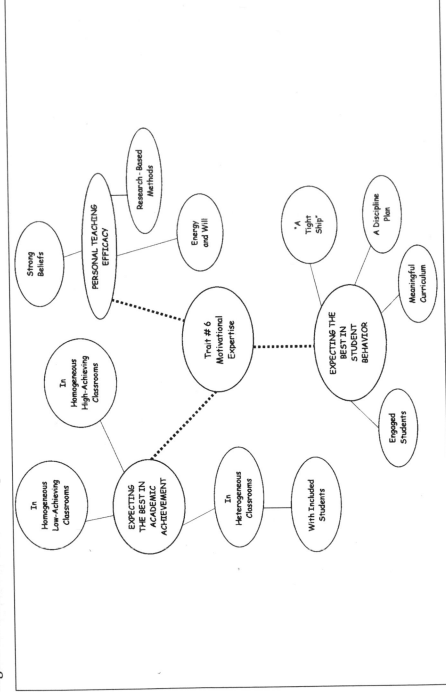

Figure 5.1. Trait 7: Instructional Effectiveness

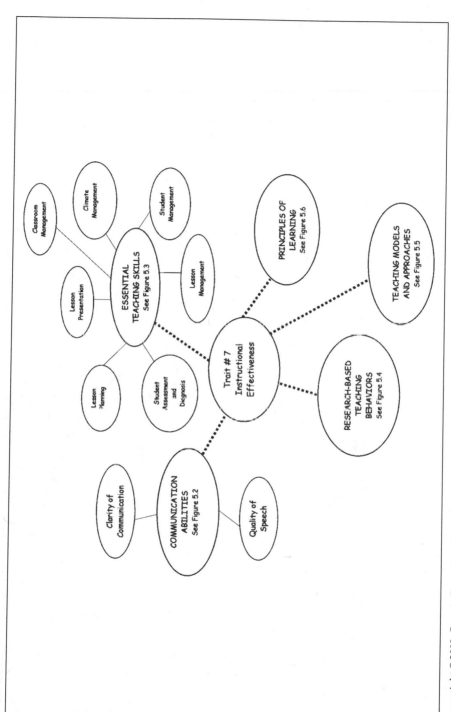

Figure 5.2. Communication Abilities

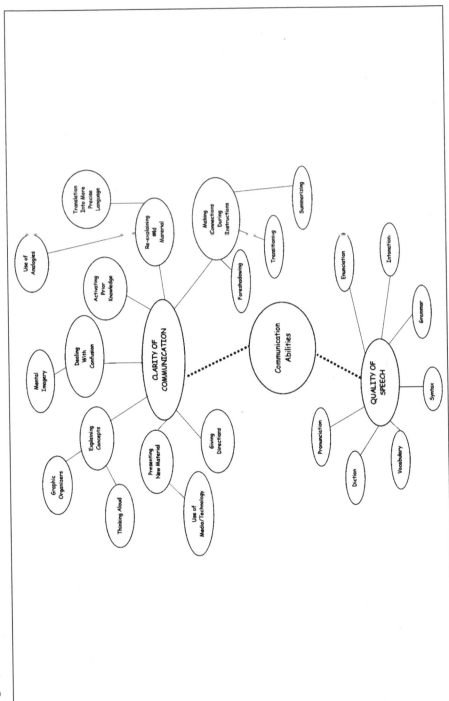

Figure 5.3. Essential Teaching Skills

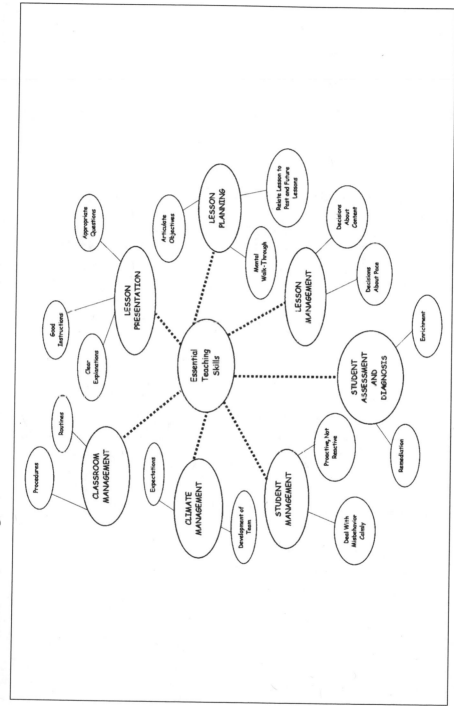

Figure 5.4. Research-Based Teaching Behaviors that Are Related to Student Achievement

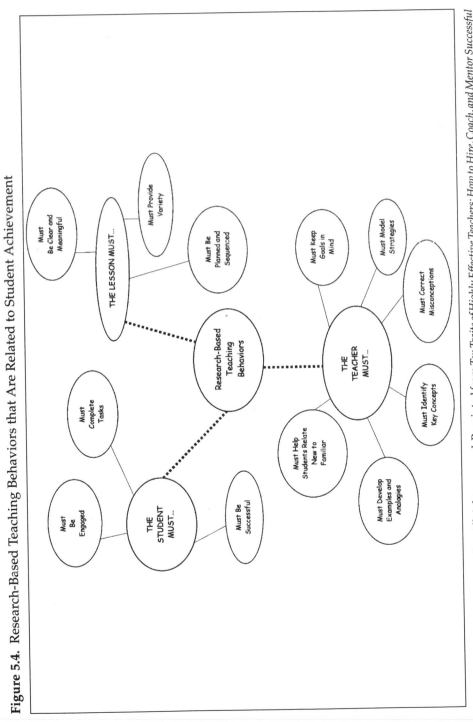

Figure 5.5. Teaching Models

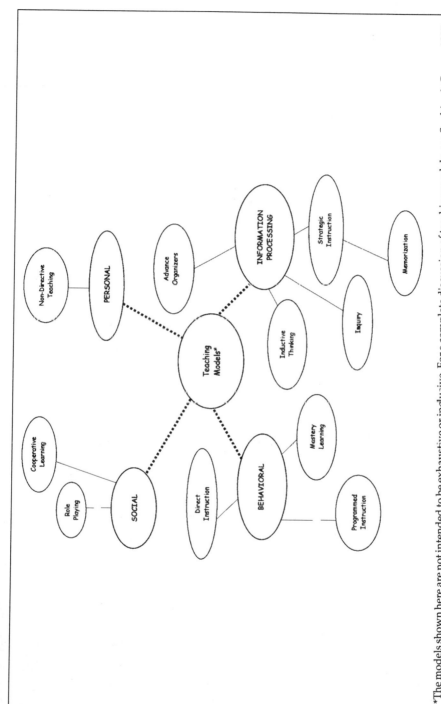

Figure 5.6. Learning Principles

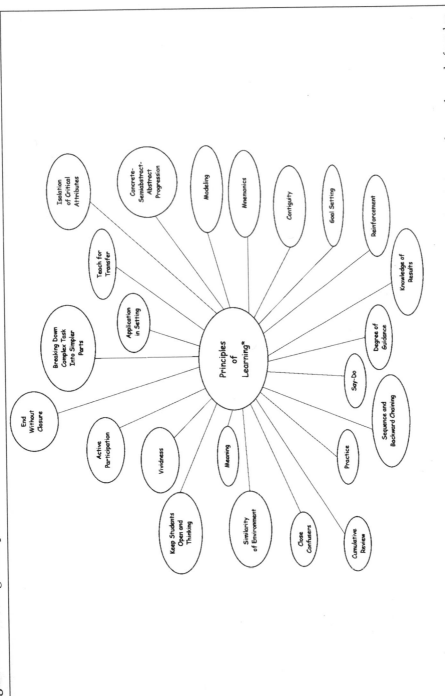

*The Principles of Learning displayed here are taken from Saphier & Gower (1997, p. 259). Definitions, descriptions, and examples can be found on pp. 237-267.

Figure 5.7. Teaching Traits That Get Results

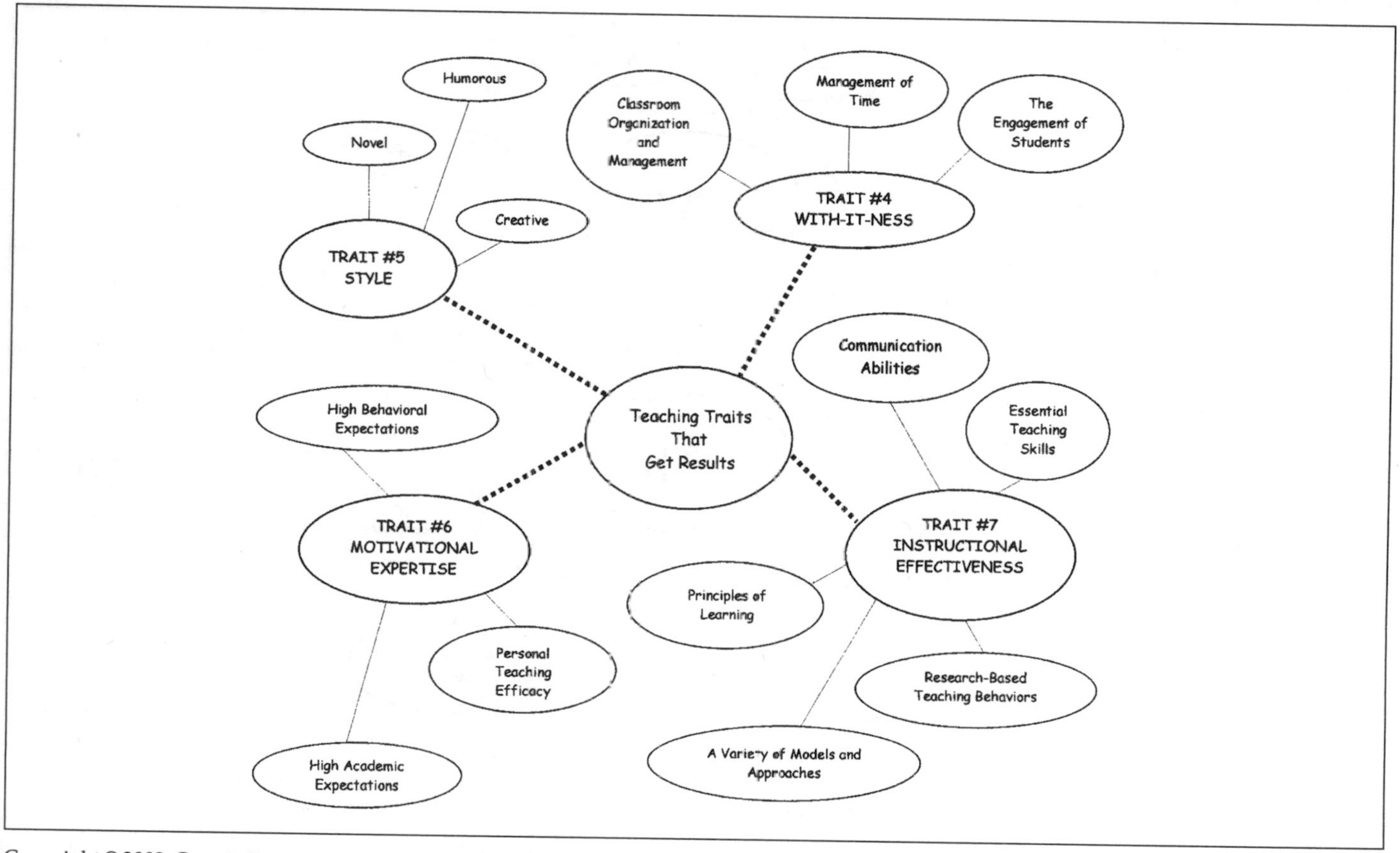

Figure 6.1. Intellectual Traits That Demonstrate Knowledge, Curiosity, and Awareness

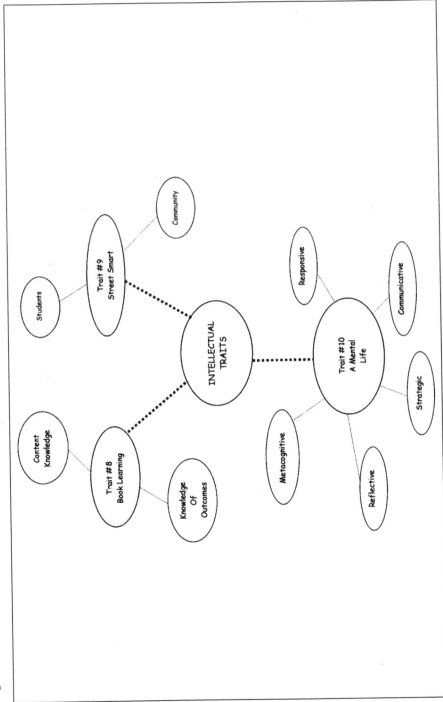

Resource B

List of Ten Traits With Definitions

Personal Traits That Indicate Character:
What a Teacher *Is*

Trait 1: Mission-Driven and Passionate

The effective teacher is mission-driven, feeling a call to teach as well as a passion to help students learn and grow.

Trait 2: Positive and Real

The highly effective teacher is positive and real, demonstrating the qualities of caring, empathy, respect, and fairness in relationships with students, parents, and colleagues.

Trait 3: A Teacher-Leader

The highly effective teacher is a teacher-leader who positively affects the lives of students, parents, and colleagues.

Teaching Traits That Get Results:
What a Teacher *Does*

Trait 4: With-It-Ness

The highly effective teacher demonstrates with-it-ness: the state of being on top of, tuned in to, aware of, and in complete control of three critical facets of classroom life:

191

1. The management and organization of the classroom

2. The engagement of students

3. The management of time

Trait 5: Style

The effective teacher exhibits his or her own unique style, bringing drama, enthusiasm, liveliness, humor, charisma, creativity, and novelty to his or her teaching.

Trait 6: Motivational Expertise

The highly effective teacher is a motivator par excellence who believes in his or her own ability to make a difference in the lives of students and relentlessly presses and pursues students to maintain the highest possible behavioral and academic standards.

Trait 7: Instructional Effectiveness

The highly effective teacher is an instructional virtuoso: a skilled communicator with a repertoire of essential abilities, behaviors, models, and principles that lead all students to learning.

Intellectual Traits That Demonstrate Knowledge, Curiosity, and Awareness

Trait 8: Book Learning

The highly effective teacher has a sound knowledge of content (the structure of the discipline) and outcomes (what the school, district, or state has determined is essential for students to know).

Trait 9: Street Smarts

The highly effective teacher has knowledge of the students, the school, and the community in which he or she is teaching and uses this knowledge to solve problems in the instructional setting.

Trait 10: A Mental Life

The highly effective teacher has a substantive thought life that includes the abilities to be the following:

1. Metacognitive: able to read one's own mental state and then assess how that state will affect one's present and future performance

2. Strategic: able to think aloud and model strategic learning for students

3. Reflective: able to think about personal teaching behaviors for the purposes of self-growth

4. Communicative: able to articulate ideas, issues, beliefs, and values about the act of teaching with colleagues, students, and parents

5. Responsive: able to flex to the changing needs and demands of the profession

Resource C

Interview Questions

Interview Questions Based on the
Ten Traits of Highly Effective Teachers

One important aspect of interviewing teacher candidates has to do with asking the right questions—questions that will disclose the person behind the application and reveal the traits that you and your team want in the teachers you hire. In the next few pages you will find over 50 interview questions—several for each of the 10 traits we identified throughout the book. You can use the list in its entirety or pick and choose questions to integrate into your current interview format.

Trait 1: Mission-Driven and Passionate

- Why did you decide to become a teacher?

- Why do you want to teach at ABC School?

- What do you think are the most important aspects of a teacher's job description?

- How have you or will you handle personal setbacks and failure in your classroom?

- Tell me about a teacher who has affected your life.

- What are your interests or passions in addition to teaching?

Trait 2: Positive and Real

- Tell me about a student (parent, or colleague) with whom you have had a difficult time getting along and how you managed to work through this problem.

- In what ways have you or would you demonstrate caring for the students in your classroom(s)?

- What does *empathy* mean to you? Describe how being empathetic might look in your relationships with students and parents.

- What does it mean to be a "fair" teacher? Give specific examples of how you would be fair in your classroom.

- What do you believe to be the most important personal quality or trait that you bring to the profession of teaching?

Trait 3: A Teacher-Leader

- Describe a position of leadership that you have held and tell us what you were able to accomplish in that position.

- How will you get your students to do things that they don't want to do (e.g., homework, follow instructions in the classroom, etc.)?

- How do you think you would like to become involved in the life of the school?

- How will you work with children, parents, or colleagues who are difficult and demanding?

- What will you do to involve the parents of your students in the educational process and life of your classroom?

Trait 4: With-It-Ness

- What do you think are the most important things to do with your students during the first day of school? The first week of school?

- What strategies or tricks do you use to make every minute count for learning in your classroom?

- When you have a single student or a group of students who aren't paying attention, what are some things you might do to get their attention? (If the candidate mentions attention-getting techniques that are authoritative in nature, probe for some moves that are more positive and have the potential for relationship building.)

Trait 5: Style

- What role does humor play in your teaching?

- If I were to ask one of your best friends to describe something unique about you, what would that individual have to say?

- How would you describe your teaching style?

Trait 6: Motivational Expertise

- Present the following true/false statements to the candidate and ask for written responses to each one. Ask him or her to provide specific examples from personal experience.

    When it comes right down to it, a teacher really can't do much because most of a student's motivation and performance depends on his or her home environment. (If the candidate answers true to this statement, he or she may lack a sense of efficacy. If the candidate answers false, he or she likely has a strong belief in his or her ability to make a difference.)

    If I really try hard, I can get through to even the most difficult or unmotivated students. (If a candidate qualifies this statement with a "yes, but . . . ," the teacher may lack a sense of efficacy. If a candidate answers yes, he or she likely has a strong belief in his or her ability to make a difference. (Berman et al., 1977).

- How would you handle a student who is not completing homework assignments and has failed the last two quizzes?

- What do *high expectations* mean to you? How do you communicate high expectations to the students in your classroom?

- Should a teacher have the same expectations for every student? Tell me how what you believe about this would work or look in your classroom.

Trait 7: Instructional Effectiveness

■ What do you believe are the most critical teaching skills? What is your strongest teaching skill? How would I see evidence of that if I were to observe your teaching? What teaching skill(s) are you working to strengthen? How are you doing that?

■ Tell me about a lesson you developed that successfully achieved a learning objective for most of your students. How did you follow up that lesson for the students who "didn't get it"?

■ How do you build meaning into a lesson for students?

■ Tell me about a lesson that you taught in which things did not go particularly well. What did you do in response to this instructional breakdown?

■ There are many different ways you can choose to present a lesson. How do you decide what approach might be the best one to use?

■ With which teaching approach(es) do you feel most comfortable? What teaching methods would you like to become more adept at using?

Trait 8: Book Learning

■ Tell me about your personal library. What books are you reading right now? For pleasure? In your discipline?

■ What books would you recommend to your students?

■ How many books do you think students should read during the school year?

■ Do you enjoy reading?

■ Tell me about your own personal learning style. How does that influence your teaching? How do you model learning for your students?

■ How will you use the library in your teaching?

■ How do you decide what to teach in your classroom?

Trait 9: Street Smarts

- What would you like to know about our school, our students, and our community that would help you to be a better teacher here?

- In what kind of setting did you do your student teaching?

- In what other kinds of settings have you worked as a volunteer or gone to school yourself?

- Have you ever lived in another country for any period of time? What cultural differences did you experience and how did you cope with those differences?

- Do you speak any other languages besides English?

Trait 10: A Mental Life

- What does *metacognitive* mean to you in the context of your teaching?

- What cognitive strategies (learning strategies) do you feel the students at your grade level or in your discipline need to know? How would you go about teaching those strategies?

- Think of an instance in your teaching experience to date when you have been flexible. What were the conditions and the state of your mind that enabled you to be flexible? Think of an instance where you stood your ground and refused to bend or change. What were the conditions and state of your mind that caused you to take the stance you did?

- What kind of teacher do you want to be remembered for being by your students?

Resource D

Recommended Reading List

Recommended Reading List to Enrich
Your Study of the Ten Traits

Trait 1: Mission-Driven and Passionate

Fried, R. L. (1995). *The Passionate Teacher: A Practical Guide.* Boston: Beacon.
Kohl, H. (1984). *Growing Minds: On Becoming a Teacher.* New York: Harper & Row.

Trait 2: Positive and Real

Banner, J. M., & Cannon, H. C. (1997). *The Elements of Teaching.* New Haven, CT: Yale University Press.
Kottler, J. A., & Zehm, S. J. (2000). *On Being a Teacher: The Human Dimension.* Thousand Oaks, CA: Corwin Press.

Trait 3: A Teacher-Leader

Bolman, L. G., & Deal, T. E. (1994). *Becoming a Teacher Leader: From Isolation to Collaboration.* Thousand Oaks, CA: Corwin Press.
Gardner, J. W. (1989). *On Leadership.* New York: Free Press.
Meichenbaum, D., & Biemiller, A. (1998). *Nurturing Independent Learners: Helping Students Take Charge of Their Learning.* Cambridge, MA: Brookline Books.
Pellicer, L. O., & Anderson, L. W. (1995). *A Handbook for Teacher Leaders.* Thousand Oaks, CA: Corwin Press.

Trait 4: With-It-Ness

Saphier, J., & Gower, R. (1997). *The Skillful Teacher: Building Your Teaching Skills*. Acton, MA: Research for Better Teaching.

Wong, H. K., & Wong, R. T. (1998). *How to Be an Effective Teacher: The First Days of School*. Mountain View, CA: Harry K. Wong Publications.

Trait 5: Style

Albom, M. (1997). *Tuesdays With Morrie: An Old Man, a Young Man, and Life's Greatest Lesson*. New York: Doubleday.

Codell, E. (1999). *Educating Esme: Diary of a Teacher's First Year*. Chapel Hill, NC: Algonquin Books of Chapel Hill.

Johnson, L. A. (1995). *The Girls in the Back of the Class*. New York: St. Martin's.

Mathews, J. (1988). *Escalante: The Best Teacher in America*. New York: Henry Holt.

Trait 6: Motivational Expertise

Kameenui, E. J., & Darch, C. B. (1995). *Instructional Classroom Management: A Proactive Approach to Behavior Management*. White Plains, NY: Longman.

Meichenbaum, D., & Biemiller, A. (1998). *Nurturing Independent Learners*. Cambridge, MA: Brookline Books.

Saphier, J., & Gower, R. (1997). *The Skillful Teacher: Building Your Teaching Skills*. Acton, MA: Research for Better Teaching.

Trait 7: Instructional Effectiveness

Hunter, M. (1967). *Teach More—Faster*. Thousand Oaks, CA: Corwin Press.

Hunter, M. (1982). *Mastery Teaching*. Thousand Oaks, CA: Corwin Press.

Joyce, B., & Weil, M. (1996). *Models of Teaching*. Boston: Allyn & Bacon.

Saphier, J., & Gower, R. (1997). *The Skillful Teacher: Building Your Teaching Skills*. Acton, MA: Research for Better Teaching.

Trait 8: Book Learning

English, F. (1992). *Deciding What to Teach and Test.*Thousand Oaks, CA: Corwin Press.

Palmer, P. J. (1998). *The Courage to Teach: Exploring the Inner Landscape of a Teacher's Life.* San Francisco: Jossey-Bass.

Trait 9: Street Smarts

Delpit, L. (1995). *Other People's Children: Cultural Conflict in the Classroom.* New York: The New Press.

Eckert, P. (1989). *Jocks and Burnouts: Social Categories and Identity in High School.* New York: Teachers College Press.

Finn, P. J. (1999). *Literacy With an Attitude: Educating Working-Class Children in Their Own Self-Interest.* Albany: State University of New York Press.

Freire, P. (1998). *Teachers as Cultural Workers: Letters to Those Who Dare to Teach.* New York: Westview Press.

Heath, S. B. (1983). *Ways With Words: Language, Life and Work in Communities and Classrooms.* Cambridge, UK: Cambridge University Press.

Kozol, J. (1991). *Savage Inequalities: Children in America's Schools.* New York: Crown Publishers.

Payne, R. (1998). *A Framework for Understanding Poverty.* Highlands, TX: RFT Publishing Co.

Trait 10: A Mental Life

Ghaye, A., & Ghaye, K. (1998). *Teaching and Learning Through Critical Reflective Practice.* London: David Fulton Publishers.

Palmer, P. J. (1998). *The Courage to Teach: Exploring the Inner Landscape of a Teacher's Life.* San Francisco: Jossey-Bass.

Resource E

Exercises to Energize Experienced Teachers

This resource contains questions and exercises to energize experienced teachers. They can be used by individuals who wish to reflect on their own teaching careers or they can be used as group exercises in a school setting. Some are appropriate for small groups and others will work well with an entire faculty.

Trait 1: Mission-Driven and Passionate

- How has your mission as a teacher changed over the years?

- Think about and then describe your personal metaphor for teaching. For example, do you see yourself as a mother or father to your students, a coach, a sage on the stage, a guide on the side, a facilitator, a midwife, a gardener, a counselor, or a doctor? Perhaps your personal metaphor is one that is not listed. Use your creativity to come up with a metaphor that fits your approach to teaching.[1]

- What do you do to keep your personal passion and excitement for teaching alive?

- Share an example of a long-term reward that has come to you from teaching.

- Relate an example of how you have empowered a particular student or shared your own personal interests with your class.

- Why did you become a teacher?

- What did you hope to accomplish as a teacher?

- What is it that you have been able to do, and are now doing, as a teacher?

- What do you see in your future as a teacher?

Trait 2: Positive and Real

- What do you believe to be the most important personal quality or trait that you bring to the profession of teaching?

- Choose a student in your class (or classes) with whom you have a personality clash or with whom you have not bonded or connected. Does this student threaten your classroom control in some way? Does he or she show signs of disrespect? Does he or she make you feel guilty because you can't meet his or her needs? Reflect on the characteristics of the "real and personal" teacher (respect, caring, empathy, and fairness). Then, list two actions, behaviors, or both that you will intentionally take on a daily basis to show that you respect the student, care for the student, and have an understanding and appreciation for what the student's life is like.

- Choose a parent with whom you have a personality clash or with whom you have not connected. Does this parent threaten you in some way? Does he or she show signs of disrespect? Does he or she make you feel guilty because you can't meet his or her needs? Reflect on the characteristics of the "real and personal" teacher (respect, caring, and empathy). Then, list two actions that you will intentionally take on a weekly basis to show that you respect the parent, care for the parent, and have an understanding and appreciation for what the parent's life is like (McEwan, 1998a).

Trait 3: A Teacher-Leader

- How would you describe your leadership style with students? Parents? Colleagues? Do you feel equally comfortable with each group? How might you enhance your skills and leadership opportunities with parents, colleagues, and students?

- Think about your effectiveness in providing leadership to parents. Do you take opportunities when presented to teach parents how to help their students at home? Do you "tell the truth in love" to parents regarding their children, or do you take the easy way out and gloss over problems and academic deficiencies that a student may have? How would you rate your ability to interact with parents? Do you make positive phone calls to parents at least two or three times weekly?

- Evaluate your personal growth as a teacher-leader among your colleagues. Which of the activities related to leadership among colleagues (e.g., those listed in the section in Chapter 2 titled "Leading Colleagues") have engaged your time during this school year? If you have not been involved in this way, what do you think is holding you back?

- Ask some students to volunteer to meet with you during a study hall or free period to design a simple, one-page, informal evaluation of how students think the class is doing and what they think might be improved. Try to put the questions in a positive tone. Then let them administer and tabulate the results, and announce that you will repeat this in 5 or 6 weeks to see how things are then (Fried, 1995).

Trait 4: With-It-Ness

- Think about your students and long-term learning objectives in the light of Jason's story (the student in reading class from Chapter 3). Where do you typically lose time in the school day? Interruptions from others? (Work with your administration to crack down on these time robbers.) Interruptions from yourself? (Monitor the number of times you stray off course during the school day and seek to reduce these self-interruptions.) Interruptions from students? (Step back and examine whether you have taught your students the procedures, routines, and expectations that will eliminate repetitive questions and problems and create a smooth-running classroom.) What other steps might you take to ensure that you use time more wisely?[2]

- What is your typical response to a student who is not paying attention? Do you overuse attention-getting moves that are authoritative and critical in nature? Do you use a wide variety of moves to keep students "guessing" and on-task? Do you use positive and affirming attention-getting moves for high-achieving students and more critical or negative moves for low-achieving students?

■ Team with other teachers to develop grade-level or departmental opening day (or week) lessons that standardize procedures (e.g., homework, paper setup, etc.). The standardization of classroom routines is particularly helpful in departmentalized settings where students move from teacher to teacher. If each teacher has the same set of expectations and routines, students will spend less time in transition and more time on-task and all teachers will have more time for instruction.

■ Do you believe that a teacher can learn with-it-ness, or is it just something you have? What advice would you give to brand-new teachers trying to become more with-it?

Trait 5: Style

■ Describe your teaching style. How has it evolved over the years? How do you use this style to engage your students?

■ What do you believe the role of humor to be in being an effective teacher? How do you use humor in your classroom? What advice would you give to a new teacher regarding that familiar rule "Don't Smile Until Christmas"?

■ In what ways do you allow students to get a glimpse of you as someone with a life outside of school? Do you find this to be an easy or difficult part of teaching?

Trait 6: Motivational Expertise

■ Obtain a copy of the instrument to evaluate your personal efficacy level from T. Guskey, *Evaluating Professional Development* (2000, p. 143). This instrument evaluates teachers' perceptions of their personal influence in teaching and learning as well as teachers' perceptions of the influence of external factors. Respondents indicate their agreement or disagreement with 21 statements on a 6-point scale ranging from *Strongly Agree* to *Strongly Disagree*.

■ Use the list of behaviors from Brophy and Good (1974) included in Chapter 4 to evaluate your behaviors toward high-achieving versus low-achieving students. Pair with a colleague who has also evaluated his or her own teaching performance and then take turns observing in each other's classroom to chart the frequency of these behaviors. Discuss your findings and develop a plan to eliminate differential treatment of students.

Trait 7: Instructional Effectiveness

■ *Improved Instruction* by Madeline Hunter (1976) contains a series of 10 inservice meetings dealing with such topics as "Extending Students' Thinking," "Designing Effective Practice," and "Teaching to Achieve Independent Learners." The lesson plans can be used to structure small learning groups or even a faculty meeting. Join with a small group of teachers to present this lesson to your faculty.

■ Use the jigsaw method of cooperative learning to share a variety of teaching models or approaches with a small group (e.g., role-playing, buzz groups, brainstorming, or small-group discussion). Divide the faculty into groups of five. Assign a different teaching model to each member of each group. Each will be responsible for teaching the critical attributes of their assigned model to the members of their small group. At the conclusion of the jigsaw exercise every participant will have been introduced to five new models, one they studied and presented, and four which they learned about from others. This process could also be used to share five different kinds of cognitive strategies (Pressley, 1995).

■ Obtain a copy of the videotape *Supervision and Practice* (Glenn, Sullivan, & Glanz, 2000). Choose teaching sequences in the tape that are appropriate to your level (e.g., elementary, middle, or high school) and watch them as a grade level, department, or faculty. Divide into small groups and identify aspects of instructional effectiveness that have been discussed in this chapter in the taped lesson. The purchase of commercial videotape is essential to the successful implementation of this activity.

Trait 8: Book Learning

■ List the courses or workshops you have attended in the last 2 years that have contributed to your content knowledge. What frustrations do you feel regarding staying in touch with your discipline?

■ List one book related to your field of teaching you have read during the past year. What changes in your thinking or practice resulted from your reading? What books would you read if you had more time?

■ Ask a small group of fellow teachers to form a short-term book club (i.e., the group will commit to meet weekly or semiweekly for 6 to 8 weeks). Choose a book related to education.

■ Do you have a reading list of books that you never fail to recommend to your students? What are some of their titles? Prepare a bibliography to either give to parents or to hand out to students containing your recommendations. Offer an award or honor to those students who read the books.

■ What would you say is the most influential book in your discipline? Who is your favorite author?

■ Imagine that because of a sudden budgetary crisis, your school is closing in 2 weeks and you have to teach an entire semester's worth of material in that time. What material will you focus on? Take that short list and try to build an entire semester-length course around only what's on it (Fried, 1995).

■ Locate 6 to 10 students who took one of your courses a year or two ago (try to find students who got a grade of B or better). Ask them what they remember from the course: What ideas or skills or knowledge are they using now or do they feel will be very important to them in the future? If they are willing, let them take the final exam over again (or a shortened version of it), anonymously. Have them trade exam books with one another and score the test. Talk about what has remained with them and, especially, what they would have liked to learn more about (Fried, 1995).

Trait 9: Street Smarts

■ How would you describe the culture of your students, school, and community to someone who had just joined the faculty? What are the unspoken or hidden rules that regulate your communication with one another?

Trait 10: A Mental Life

■ Invite into class one of your own favorite teachers or someone in your field whose work you especially admire. Tell your students about it in advance, so they can read something by or about that person and think of some questions to ask. When your guest arrives, and after a brief introduction, find a seat in your classroom and join the discussion (so that your students can see you in a learner's role) (Fried, 1995).

Notes

1. Robert Simola, in his book *Teaching in the Real World* (1996), suggests two other metaphors for teachers—a performer in a three-ring circus or an 800-pound gorilla in the jungle. He advises that teachers choose the gorilla role. "You will seldom have any problems because all your students know the immediate consequence of disturbing the 800-pound gorilla living in their midst" (p. xv).

2. Following a visit by Jane Stallings (our teachers called her the time-on-task lady) to our district, the staff at Lincoln School engaged in a systematic effort to determine how effectively we were using time. Teachers were shocked to discover how much allocated time was wasted on meaningless administrivia; how poorly engaged many students were during the lessons they had worked so hard to prepare; and how miniscule the success rate was for still other students who appeared to be on-task. This exercise created a new awareness of the importance of time at every level. We eliminated intercom announcements, changed the scheduling for special teachers to allow more uninterrupted time for reading instruction, and began to treat the "lesson as sacred," much like teachers in Japan routinely do.

References

Agne, K. (1999). Caring: The way of the master teacher. In R. P. Lipka & T. M. Brinthaupt (Eds.), *The role of self in teacher development* (pp. 165-188). Albany: State University of New York Press.

Albom, M. (1997). *Tuesdays with Morrie: An old man, a young man, and life's greatest lesson.* New York: Doubleday.

Anderson, L. W. (1975). Student involvement in learning and school achievement. *California Journal of Educational Research, 26*(3), 53-62.

Andrews, R. (2000, November 29). More action, less abstraction. *Education Week,* 37.

Armor, D., Conry-Oseguera, P., Cox, M., King, N., McDonnell, L., Pascal, A., Pauly, E., & Zellman, G. (1976). *Analysis of the School Preferred Reading Program in selected Los Angeles minority schools* (Report No. R-2007-LAUSD). Santa Monica, CA: RAND. (ERIC Document Reproduction Service No. ED 130 243)

Ashton, P. T., & Webb, R. B. (1986). *Making a difference: Teachers' sense of efficacy and student achievement.* New York: Longman.

Aspy, D. N., & Roebuck, F. N. (1977). *Kids don't learn from people they don't like.* Amherst, MA: Human Resource Development Press.

Ayers, W. (1993). *To teach: The journey of a teacher.* New York: Teachers College Press.

Banner, J. M., & Cannon, H. C. (1997). *The elements of teaching.* New Haven: Yale University Press.

Barr, A. S., & Emans, L. M. (1930, September). What qualities are prerequisites to success in teaching? *Nation's Schools, 6*(9), 60-64.

Barzun, J. (1991). *Begin here: The forgotten conditions of teaching and learning.* Chicago: University of Chicago Press.

Bellon, J. (1988, November-December). The dimensions of leadership. *Vocational Education Journal, 63,* 29-31.

Berliner, D. (1985). Effective classroom teaching: The necessary but not sufficient condition for developing exemplary schools. In G. Austin & H. Garber (Eds.), *Research on exemplary schools* (pp. 127-154). Orlando, FL: Academic Press.

Berman, P., McLaughlin, M., Bass, G., Pauly, E., & Zellman, G. (1977). *Federal programs supporting educational change: Vol. 7. Factors affecting implementation and continuation.* Santa Monica, CA: RAND. (ERIC Document Reproduction Service No. ED 140 432)

Blair, J. (1999, September 6). States strive to lure retired teachers [Online]. *Education Week.* Retrieved March 2001 from the World Wide Web: http://www.educationweek.org

Blair, J. (2000, August 2). Districts wooing teachers with bonuses, incentives [Online]. *Education Week.* Retrieved March 2001 from the World Wide Web: www.educationweek.org

Blase, J., & Blase, J. (1998). *Handbook of instructional leadership: How really good principals promote teaching and learning.* Thousand Oaks, CA: Corwin Press.

Blase, J., & Kirby, P. (2000). *Bringing out the best in teachers.* Thousand Oaks, CA: Corwin Press.

Bloom, B. S. (1974, September). Time and learning. *American Psychologist, 29,* 682-688.

Bolman, L., & Deal, T. (1994). *Becoming a teacher leader: From isolation to collaboration.* Thousand Oaks, CA: Corwin Press.

Bolt, R. (1962). *A man for all seasons.* New York: Basic Books.

Borich, G. D. (1993). *Clearly outstanding: Making each day count in your classroom.* Boston: Allyn & Bacon.

Borich, G. D. (2000). *Effective teaching methods* (4th ed.). Upper Saddle River, NJ: Merrill.

Boser, U. (2000). A picture of the teacher pipeline: Baccalaureate and beyond. *Quality counts 2000: Who should teach?* Bethesda, MD: Editorial Projects in Education.

Brock, B. (1990). Profile of the beginning teacher. *Momentum, 21*(4), 54-57.

Brock, B. L., & Grady, M. L. (1997). *From first-year to first-rate: Principals guiding beginning teachers.* Thousand Oaks, CA: Corwin Press.

Brooks, D. M. (1985). The first day of school. *Educational Leadership, 41*(5), 76-78.

Brooks, J. G., & Brooks, M. G. (1993). *In search of understanding: The case for constructivist classrooms.* Alexandria, VA: Association for Supervision and Curriculum Development.

Brophy, J. (Ed.). (1989). *Advances in research on teaching* (Vol. 1). Greenwich, CT: JAI.

Brophy, J. E., & Good, T. L. (1974). *Teacher-student relationships: Causes and consequences.* New York: Holt, Rinehart & Winston.

Brophy, J. E., & Good, T. L. (1986). Teacher behavior and student achievement. In M. C. Wittrock (Ed.), *Handbook of research on teaching* (3rd ed., pp. 328-375). Upper Saddle River, NJ: Merrill/Prentice Hall.

Brown, R., Pressley, M., Van Meter, P., & Schuder, T. (1996). A quasi-experimental validation of transactional strategies instruction with low-achieving second-grade readers. *Journal of Educational Psychology, 88*(1), 18-37

Bullough, R. V. (1989). *First-year teacher: A case study.* New York: Teachers College Press.

Burke, R. W., & Nierenberg, I. (1998). In search of the inspirational in teachers and teaching. *Journal for a Just and Caring Education, 4*(3), 336-355.

Caldwell, J. H., Huitt, W. G., & Graeber, A. O. (1982). Time spent in learning. *Elementary School Journal, 82*(5), 371-480.

California Commission on Teacher Credentialing and the California Department of Education. (1998). *Support provider guidebook.* Sacramento, CA: Author.

Chickering, A. (1977). *Experience and learning: An introduction to experiential learning.* New York: Change Magazine Press.

Codell, E. (1999). *Educating Esme: Diary of a teacher's first year.* Chapel Hill, NC: Algonquin Books of Chapel Hill.

Coleman, J. (1966). *Equality of educational opportunity.* Washington, DC: Office of Education, U.S. Department of Health, Education, and Welfare.

Collay, M., Dunlap, D., Enloe, W., & Gagnon, G. (1998). *Learning circles: Creating conditions for professional development.* Thousand Oaks, CA: Corwin Press.

Collins, M., & Tamarkin, C. (1982). *Marva Collins' way.* Los Angeles: Tarcher.

Coppedge, F. L., & Shreck, P. (1988). Teachers as helpers: The qualities students prefer. *Clearing House, 62*(1), 37-40.

Covey, S. (1990). *Principle-centered leadership.* New York: Simon & Schuster.

Cowper, W. (1968). In E. Beck (Ed.), *Bartlett's familiar quotations* (14th ed., p. 458b). Boston: Little, Brown. (Original work published 1785)

Darling-Hammond, Linda. (2000). Teacher quality and student achievement: A review of state policy evidence [Online]. *Education Policy Analysis Archives, 8*(1). Retrieved March 2001 from the World Wide Web: www.olam.ed.asu.edu/epaa/v8n1

DeBono, Edward. (1999). *Six thinking hats.* Boston: Little, Brown.

Delisle, J. (1995, November/December). Too smart to teach [Online]. *Teacher Magazine.* Retrieved February 2001 from the World Wide Web: www.educationweek.org

Delpit, L. (1986). Skills and other dilemmas of a progressive black educator. *Harvard Educational Review, 56*(4), 379-385.

Delpit, L. (1988). The silenced dialogue: Power and pedagogy in educating other people's children. *Harvard Educational Review, 58*(3), 280-298.

Delpit, L. (1995). *Other people's children: Cultural conflict in the classroom.* New York: The New Press.

Dollase, R. (1992). *Voices of beginning teachers: Visions and realities.* New York: Teachers College Press.

Duffey, R. V. (1973). Teacher as reader. *Reading Teacher, 27,*132-133.

Duffey, R. V. (1974, October/November). *Elementary school teachers' reading.* Paper presented at the annual meeting of the College Reading Association, Bethesda, MD. (ERIC Document Reproduction Service No. ED 098 554)

DuFour, R. (1991). *The principal as staff developer.* Bloomington, IN: National Educational Service.

Dunkin, M. J., & Biddle, B. J. (1974). *The study of teaching.* New York: Holt, Rinehart & Winston.

Eckert, P. (1989). *Jocks and burnouts: Social categories and identity in the high school.* New York: Teachers College Press.

Einhardt, G., Putnam, R. T., Stein, M. K., & Baxter, J. (1991). Where subject knowledge matters. In J. Brophy (Ed.), *Advances in research on teaching* (Vol. 2, pp. 87-113). Greenwich, CT: JAI.

English, F. (1992). *Deciding what to teach and test.* Thousand Oaks, CA: Corwin Press.

Ennis, C. D. (1998). Shared expectations: Creating a joint vision for urban schools. In J. Brophy (Ed.), *Advances in research on teaching: Expectations in the classroom* (pp. 151-182). Greenwich, CT: JAI.

Ferguson, R. F. (1998). Can schools narrow the black-white test score gap? In C. Jencks & M. Phillips, (Eds.), *The black-white test score gap* (pp. 318-374). Washington, DC: Brookings Institution.

Ferguson, R. F., & Ladd, H. F. (1996). *Holding schools accountable: Performance based reform in education.* Washington, DC: Brookings Institution.

Fine, M. (1991). *Framing dropouts: Notes on the politics of an urban public high school.* Albany: State University of New York Press.

Finkel, D. L. (2000). *Teaching with your mouth shut.* Portsmouth, NH: Boynton/Cook Publishers, Inc.

Finn, P. J. (1999). *Literacy with an attitude: Educating working-class children in their own self-interest.* Albany: State University of New York Press.

Fishbaugh, M. S. (1997). *Models of collaboration.* Boston: Allyn & Bacon.

Fisher, C. W., Filby, N. N., Marliave, R. S., Cahen, L. S., Dishaw, M. M., Moore, J. E., & Berliner, D. C., (1978). *Teaching behaviors, academic learning time and student achievement* (Final Report of Phase III-B, Beginning Teacher Evaluation Study, Tech. Rep V-1). San Francisco: Far West Laboratory for Educational Research and Development.

Freire, P. (1998). *Teachers as cultural workers: Letters to those who dare to teach.* New York: Westview Press.

Fried, R. L. (1995). *The passionate teacher: A practical guide.* Boston: Beacon Press.

Friedman, T. (2001, January 9). My favorite teacher [Online]. *New York Times.* Retrieved January 2001 from the World Wide Web: http://www.nytimes.com

Fuchs, E. (1969). *Teachers talk: Views from inside city schools.* Garden City, NY: Doubleday.

Fuery, C. (1989). *Winning year one: A survival manual for first-year teachers.* Captiva, FL: Sanddollar Publications.

Fuery, C. (1994). *Discipline strategies for the bored, belligerent, and ballistic in your classroom.* Captiva, FL: Sanddollar Publications.

Fullan, M. (1990). Staff development, innovation and institutional development. In B. Joyce (Ed.), *Changing school culture through staff development* (pp. 3-25). Alexandria, VA: Association for Supervision and Curriculum Development.

Gage, N. L. (Ed.). (1963). *Handbook of research on teaching.* Chicago: Rand McNally.

Gage, N. L. (1985). *Hard gains in the soft sciences: The case of pedagogy.* Bloomington, IN: Phi Delta Kappa.

Galambos, E. C., Cornett, L. M., & Spitler, H. D. (1985). *An analysis of transcripts of teachers and arts and sciences graduates.* Atlanta, GA: Southern Regional Education Board.

Galley, M. (2001, March 7). For sale: Affordable housing for teachers. *Education Week,* 1, 16-17.

Galluzzo, G. R. (1999, May 5). Will the best and the brightest teach? [Online]. *Education Week.* Retrieved February 2001 from the World Wide Web: www.educationweek.org

Gardner, J. W. (1989). *On leadership.* New York: Free Press.

Garner, D. (1997). *Texas alternative document* [Online]. Available: www.educationnews.org/texas_alternative_document.htm [March, 2001].

Gehrke, N. (1991). Seeing our way to better helping of beginning teachers. *Educational Forum, 55,* 233-242.

Ghaye, A., & Ghaye, K. (1998). *Teaching and learning through critical reflective practice.* London: David Fulton Publishers.

Gill, V. (1998). *The ten commandments of good teaching.* Thousand Oaks, CA: Corwin Press.

Glatthorn, A. (1987). Cooperative professional development: Peer-centered options for teacher growth. *Educational Leadership, 45*(3), 31-35.

Glenn, J., Sullivan, S., & Glanz, J. (2000). *Supervision and practice* [Videotape]. Thousand Oaks, CA: Corwin Press.

Goldsberry, L. F. (1986, April). *Colleague consultation: Another case of fools rush in.* Paper presented at the annual meeting of the American Educational Research Association, San Francisco, CA.

Good, H. (2000, October 18). Epitaph for an English teacher [Online]. *Education Week.* Retrieved February 2001 from the World Wide Web: www.educationweek.org

Goodwin, A. L. (1987). Vocational choice and the realities of teaching. In F. S. Bolin & J. M. Falk (Eds.), *Teacher renewal: Professional issues, personal choices* (pp. 30-36). New York: Teachers College Press.

Guskey, T. (2000). *Evaluating professional development.* Thousand Oaks, CA: Corwin Press.

Haberman, M. (1998, March). Star teachers: What makes great teachers and why they're so important. *Instructional Leader, 11*(2), 1-9.

Hamachek, D. (1999). Effective teachers: What they do, how they do it, and the importance of self-knowledge. In R. P. Lipka & T. M. Brinthaupt (Eds.), *The role of self in teacher development* (pp. 189-224). Albany: State University of New York Press.

Harris, K. R., & Graham, S. (1996). *Making the writing process work: Strategies for composition and self-regulation.* Cambridge, MA: Brookline Books.

Heath, S. B. (1983). *Ways with words: Language, life and work in communities and classrooms.* Cambridge, UK: Cambridge University Press.

Highet, G. (1976). *The immortal profession: The joys of teaching and learning.* New York: Weyright and Talley.

Hofstadter, R. (1963). *Anti-intellectualism in American life.* New York: Knopf.

Hosford, P. (1984). The art of applying the science of education. In P. Hosford (Ed.), *Using what we know about teaching* (pp. 141-161). Alexandria, VA: Association for Supervision and Curriculum Development.

Houston, W. R., Clift, R. T., Freibert, H. J., & Warner, A. R. (1988). *Touch the future.* St. Paul, MN: West.

Howell, J. (1992). *Proverbs.* Quoted in J. Kaplan (Ed.), *Bartlett's familiar quotations* (16th ed., p. 246). (Original work published 1659). Boston: Little, Brown.

Howley, A., & Howley, C. B. (1995). The mechanisms of anti-intellectualism in the schools. In C. B. Howley, A. Howley, & E. D. Pendarvis (Eds.), *Out of our minds: Anti-intellectualism and talent development in American schooling* (pp. 44-76). New York: Teachers College Press.

Hunter, M. (1967a). *Motivation theory for teachers.* Thousand Oaks, CA: Corwin Press.

Hunter, M. (1967b). *Retention theory for teachers.* Thousand Oaks, CA: Corwin Press.

Hunter, M. (1967c). *Teach more—faster.* Thousand Oaks, CA: Corwin Press.

Hunter, M. (1971). *Teach for transfer.* Thousand Oaks, CA: Corwin Press.

Hunter, M. (1976). *Improved instruction.* Thousand Oaks, CA: Corwin Press.

Hunter, M. (1979). Teaching is decision-making. *Educational Leadership, 37*(1), 62-67.

Hunter, M. (1982). *Mastery teaching.* Thousand Oaks, CA: Corwin Press.

Hunter, M. (1984). Knowing, teaching and supervising. In P. Hosford (Ed.), *Using what we know about teaching* (pp. 169-192). Alexandria, VA: Association for Supervision and Curriculum Development.

Jackson, P. (1968). *Life in classrooms.* New York: Holt, Rinehart & Winston.

Jago, C. (2000). *With rigor for all: Teaching the classics to contemporary students.* Portland, ME: Calendar Islands Publishers.

Jago, C. (2001, February 28). Sound bites vs. sense. *Education Week,* p. 30.

James, W. (1902). *Talks to teachers on psychology: And to students on some of life's ideals.* New York: Henry Holt.

Jencks, C. S. (1972). The Coleman report and the conventional wisdom. In F. Mosteller & D. P. Moynihan (Eds.), *On equality of educational opportunity* (pp. 69-115). New York: Random House.

Jesness, J. (1998, August 5). What's wrong with bilingual education? Repair it, don't replace it [Online]. *Education Week.* Retrieved February 2001 from the World Wide Web: www.educationweek.org

Jesness, J. (1999, September 22). Ballast in the battleships of the reading wars [Online]. *Education Week.* Retrieved February 2001 from the World Wide Web: www.educationweek.org

Jesness, J. (2000a, March 22). Read two sonnets and call me in the morning [Online]. *Education Week.* Retrieved February 2001 from the World Wide Web: www.educationweek.org

Jesness, J. (2000b, November 8). You have your teacher's permission to be ignorant [Online]. *Education Week.* Retrieved February 2001 from the World Wide Web: www.educationweek.org

Johnson, L. A. (1995). *The girls in the back of the class.* New York: St. Martin's.

Johnson, M. S. (1976, February). I think my teacher is. *Learning,* 36-38.

Johnston, R. C. (2000, November 1). Chicago's efforts to recruit teachers pay off [Online]. *Education Week.* Retrieved March 2001 from the World Wide Web: www.educationweek.org

Joyce, B., & Weil, M. (1996). *Models of teaching.* Boston: Allyn & Bacon.

Kameenui, E. J., & Darch, C. B. (1995). *Instructional classroom management: A proactive approach to behavior management.* White Plains, NY: Longman.

Kameenui, E. J., & Simmons, D. C. (1990). *Designing instructional strategies: The prevention of academic learning problems.* Columbus, OH: Merrill.

Kane, P. R. (Ed.). (1991). *My first year as a teacher.* New York: Signet.

Kant, I. (1907). *Immanuel Kant's critique of pure reason: In commemoration of the centenary of its first publication* (Friedrich Max Muller, Trans.). New York: Macmillan.

Koehn, J. (1984). The silent curriculum: More than intuition. In P. Hosford (Ed.), *Using what we know about teaching* (pp. 162-163). Alexandria, VA: Association for Supervision and Curriculum Development.

Kohl, H. (1984). *Growing minds: On becoming a teacher.* New York: Harper & Row.

Kohl, H. (1998). *The discipline of hope: Learning from a lifetime of teaching.* New York: Simon & Schuster.

Kottler, J., & Zehm, S. J. (2000). *On being a teacher: The human dimension.* Thousand Oaks, CA: Corwin Press.

Kounin, J. (1970). *Discipline and group management in classrooms.* New York: Holt, Rinehart & Winston.

Kozol, J. (1991). *Savage inequalities: Children in America's schools.* New York: Crown Publishers.

Kratz, H. E. (1896, June). Characteristics of the best teachers as recognized by children. *Pedagogical Seminary, 3*(4), 413-418.

Kyriacou, C. (1991). *Essential teaching skills.* Oxford, UK: Basil Blackwell.

Lee, V. E., Smith, J. B., Perry, T. E., & Smylie, M. A. (1999, October). *Social support, academic press and student achievement: A view from the middle grades in Chicago* [Online].
Available: www.consortium-chicago.org [retrieved October 2000].

Leithwood, K. A. (1990). The principal's role in teacher development. In B. Joyce (Ed.), *Changing school culture through staff development* (pp. 71-90). Alexandria, VA: Association for Supervision and Curriculum Development.

Lewis, C., & Tsuchida, I. (1998). A lesson is like a swiftly flowing river: How research lessons improve Japanese education. *American Educator, 22*(4), 12-17, 50-52.

Lieberman, A. (1988). Expanding the leadership team. *Educational Leadership, 45*(5), 4-8.

Lieberman, A., & Miller, L. (1984). *Teachers, their world and their work.* Alexandria, VA: Association for Supervision and Curriculum Development.

Lieberman, A., & Miller, L. (1999). *Teachers transforming their world and their work.* New York: Teachers College Press.

Lightfoot, S. L. (1985, October). From a paper presented as the Maycie K. Southall Distinguished Lecture on Public Education and the Futures of Children, Vanderbilt University, Nashville, TN.

Lockyer, H. (1991). *All the teachings of Jesus.* San Francisco: HarperSanFrancisco.

Lortie, D. (1966). *Teacher socialization: The Robinson Crusoe model. The real world of the beginning teacher.* Washington, DC: National Commission on Teacher Education and Professional Standards.

Lortie, D. (1975). *Schoolteacher: A sociological study.* Chicago: University of Chicago Press.

Mager, G. M. (1992). The place of induction in becoming a teacher. In G. P. Debolt (Ed.), *Teacher induction and mentoring* (pp. 3-33). Albany: State University of New York Press.

Manatt, R. (1985, June 10). *Effective schools*. Workshop. Canton, IL.

Mathews, J. (1988). *Escalante: The best teacher in America*. New York: Henry Holt.

McEwan, E. K. (1997). *Leading your team to excellence: How to make quality decisions*. Thousand Oaks, CA: Corwin Press.

McEwan, E. K. (1998a). *How to deal with parents who are angry, troubled, afraid, or just plain crazy*. Thousand Oaks, CA: Corwin Press.

McEwan, E. K. (1998b). *Seven steps to effective instructional leadership*. Thousand Oaks, CA: Corwin Press.

McEwan, E. K. (2001). *Raising reading achievement in middle and high schools: Five simple-to-follow strategies for principals*. Thousand Oaks, CA: Corwin Press.

McKechnie, J. L. (Ed.). (1983). *Webster's new universal unabridged dictionary* (2nd ed.). New York: Simon & Schuster.

Meichenbaum, D., & Biemiller, A. (1998). *Nurturing independent learners*. Cambridge, MA: Brookline Books.

Mercier, C. D., Jordan, L., & Miller, S. P. (1994). Implications of constructivism for teaching math to students with moderate to mild disabilities. *Journal of Special Education, 28*, 290-306.

Moats, L. C. (2000). *Speech to print: Language essentials for teachers*. Baltimore: Paul H. Brookes.

Montessori, M. (1912). *The Montessori method: Scientific pedagogy as applied to child education in "The children's houses."* New York: Stokes Company.

Munson, P. J. (1991). *Winning teachers, teaching winners*. Santa Cruz, CA: Network.

Nelson, R. (2000, December 5). In J. Mathews, Teaching beyond the middle [Online]. *Washington Post*. Retrieved February 13, 2001 from the World Wide Web: www.washingtonpost.com.

Olsen, L. (1988). *Crossing the schoolhouse border: Immigrant students and the California public schools*. San Francisco: California Tomorrow.

Olson, L. (1997, February 5). Research notes [Online]. *Education Week*. Retrieved February 2001 from the World Wide Web: www. educationweek.org

Olson, L. (2000). Finding and keeping competent teachers. *Quality counts 2000: Who should teach?* Bethesda, MD: Editorial Projects in Education.

Owens, L. B. (1990, April). If you're so smart . . . [Online]. *Teacher*. Retrieved February 2001 from the World Wide Web: www. educationweek.org

Oxnard Union High School District. (2000). *A handbook for teachers new to the Oxnard Union High School District.* Oxnard, CA: Author.

Palmer, P. J. (1998). *The courage to teach: Exploring the inner landscape of a teacher's life.* San Francisco: Jossey-Bass.

Paris, S. G. (1985). Using classroom dialogues and guided practice to teach comprehension strategies. In T. L. Harris & E. J. Cooper (Eds.), *Reading, thinking and concept development* (pp. 133-146). New York: College Board Publications.

Pavlov, I. P. (1957). *Experimental psychology and other essays.* New York: Philosophical Library.

Payne, R. (1998). *A framework for understanding poverty.* Highlands, TX: RFT Publishing Co.

Peart, N. A., & Campbell, F. A. (1999). At-risk students' perceptions of teacher effectiveness. *Journal for a Just and Caring Education, 5*(3), 269-285.

Pellicer, L. O., & Anderson, L. W. (1995). *A handbook for teacher leaders.* Thousand Oaks, CA: Corwin Press.

Peters, T., & Austin, N. (1985). *A passion for excellence: The leadership difference.* New York: Random House.

Phelps, P. H. (1993). An induction ceremony for new teachers. *Clearing House, 66*(3), 154.

Porter, A. C., & Brophy, J. (1987). *Good teaching: Insights from the work of the Institute for Research on Teaching* (Occasional paper no. 14). East Lansing: The Institute for Research on Teaching, College of Education, Michigan State University.

Porter, A. C., & Brophy, J. (1988). Synthesis of research on good teaching: Insights from the work of the Institute for Research on Teaching. *Educational Leadership, 45*(8), 74-85.

Pressley, M., Burkell, J., Cariglia-Bull, T., Lysynchuk, L., McGoldrick, J. A., Schneider, B., Snyder, B., Symons, S., & Woloshyn, V. E. (1995). *Cognitive strategy instruction that really improves children's academic performance.* Cambridge, MA: Brookline Books.

Raywid, M. (1993). Finding time for collaboration. *Educational Leadership, 51*(1), 30-34.

Rim, E., & Coller, A. (1982). *In search of nonlinear process-product functions in existing schooling effects data: A reanalysis of the first-grade reading and mathematics data from the Stallings and Kaskowitz Follow-Through study.* Philadelphia: Research for Better Schools, Inc.

Rogers, C. R. (1957). The necessary and sufficient conditions of therapeutic personality change. *Journal of Consulting Psychology, 21*(1), 95-103.

Rosenblum-Lowden, R. (2000). *You have to go to school—you're the teacher.* Thousand Oaks, CA: Corwin Press.

Rosenshine, B. (1971). *Teaching behaviors and student achievement.* London: National Foundation for Education Research in England and Wales.

Rosenshine, B. (1983, March). Teaching functions in instructional programs. *The Elementary School Journal, 83*(3), 335-351.

Rosenshine, B., & Stevens, R. (1986). Teaching functions. In M. C. Wittrock (Ed.), *Handbook of research on teaching* (3rd ed., pp. 376-391). New York: Macmillan.

Ryans, D. G. (1960). *Characteristics of teachers: Their description, comparison and appraisal.* Washington, DC: American Council on Education.

Sanders, W. L., & Rivers, J. C. (1996). *Cumulative and residual effects of teachers on future student academic achievement.* Knoxville: University of Tennessee Value Added Research and Assessment Center.

Saphier, J., & Gower, R. (1967). *The skillful teacher: Building your teaching skills.* Carlisle, MA: Research for Better Teaching.

Saphier, J., & Gower, R. (1997). *The skillful teacher: Building your teaching skills.* Acton: MA: Research for Better Teaching.

Sarason, S. B. (1971). *The culture of the school and the problem of change.* Boston: Allyn & Bacon.

Scheidecker, D., & Freeman, W. (1999). *Bringing out the best in kids: How legendary teachers motivate kids.* Thousand Oaks, CA: Corwin Press.

Schlechty, P. C. (1990). *Schools for the 21st century.* San Francisco: Jossey-Bass.

Schlechty, P. C., & Vance, V. S. (1981). Do academically able teachers leave education? The North Carolina case. *Phi Delta Kappan, 63*(2), 106, 112.

Seeskin, K. (1986). *A study in the Socratic Method.* Albany, NY: State University of New York.

Serow, R. C. (1994). Called to teach: A study of highly motivated preservice teachers. *The Journal of Research and Development in Education, 27*(2), 65-72.

Shaker, P. (2001, January 10). Listening to the music of teaching. *Education Week,* pp. 53-54.

Shea, C. M. (1992). Search for a teacher renewal philosophy. In A. G. Rud & W. P. Oldendorf (Eds.), *A place for teacher renewal: Challenging the intellect, creating educational reform* (pp. 1-24). New York: Teachers College Press.

Shimahara, N. K. (1998). The Japanese model of professional development: Teaching as a craft. *Teaching and Teacher Education, 14,* 451-462.

Short, P. M., & Rinehart, J. S. (1992). School participant empowerment scale: Assessment of the level of empowerment within the school environment. *Educational and Psychological Measurement, 52,* 951-960.

Shulman, L. S. (1987). Knowledge and teaching: Foundations of the new reform. *Harvard Educational Review, 57*(1), 1-22.

Shulman, L. (1989). Teaching alone, learning together: Needed agendas for the new reforms. In T. Sergiovanni & J. Moore (Eds.), *Schooling for tomorrow: Directing reforms to issues that count* (pp. 166-187). Boston: Allyn & Bacon.

Simola, R. (1996). *Teaching in the real world.* Englewood, CO: Teachers Ideas Press.

Skinner, B. F. (1953). *Science and human behavior.* New York: Macmillan.

Smith, L., & Land, M. (1981). Low-inference verbal behaviors related to teacher clarity. *Journal of Classroom Interactions, 17*(1), 37-42.

Smylie, M. A. (1989). Teachers' views of the effectiveness of the sources of learning to teach. *The Elementary School Journal, 89*(5), 543-558.

Soar, R., & Soar, R. (1979). Emotional climate and management. In P. Peterson & H. Wallberg (Eds.), *Research on teaching: Concepts, findings, and implications* (pp. 97-119). Berkeley, CA: McCutchen.

Sparks, R., & Lipka, R. P. (1992). Characteristics of master teachers: personality factors, self-concept, locus of control, and pupil ideology. *Journal of Personnel and Evaluation in Education, 5,* 303-311.

Stallings, J. A. (1980, December). Allocated academic learning time revisited, or beyond time on task. *Educational Researcher, 9*(12), pp. 9, 11.

Stallings, J. A. (1985). *Using time effectively in the classroom.* Unpublished paper. Peabody Center for Effective Teaching. Vanderbilt University, Nashville, TN.

Stigler, J. W., & Hiebert, J. (1997, January). Understanding and improving classroom mathematics instruction: An overview of the TIMSS video study. *Phi Delta Kappan, 79*(1), pp. 14-21.

Stigler, J. W., & Hiebert, J. (1999). *The teaching gap.* New York: The Free Press.

Sullivan, S., & Glanz, J. (2000). *Supervision that improves teaching: Strategies and techniques.* Thousand Oaks, CA: Corwin Press.

Taylor, L. (1995). A handy workable picture file. *Perspectives in Education and Deafness, 13*(5), 2-4.

Taylor, L. (2001). What teachers wish parents knew about working as partners. *Michigan Learning, 3*(4), 6.

Taylor-Dunlop, K., & Norton, M. M. (1997). Voices of at-risk adolescents: Out of the mouths of babes. *Clearing House, 70*(5), 274-279.

Teddlie, C., & Stringfield, S. (1993). *Schools make a difference: Lessons learned from a 10-year study of school effects.* New York: Teachers College Press.

Thorndike, E. L. (1913). *Educational psychology.* New York: Teachers College Press.

Traina, R. P. (1999, January 20). What makes a good teacher [Online]. *Education Week.* Retrieved January 2001 from the World Wide Web: www.educationweek.org

Troen, V., & Boles, K. (1994, February). A time to lead. *Teacher Magazine,* 40-41.

U.S. Department of Education. (1999). *Attaining Excellence: A TIMMS resource kit (#065-000-01013-5).* Pittsburgh, PA: U.S. Government Printing Office.

Valverde, X. (1982). The self-evolving supervisor. In T. Sergiovanni (Ed.), *Supervision of teaching* (pp. 81-89). Alexandria, VA: Association for Supervision and Curriculum Development.

Vance, V. S., & Schlechty, P. C. (1982). The distribution of academic ability in the teaching force: Policy implications. *Phi Delta Kappan, 64*(1), 22-27.

van der Sijde, P. (1990). The effects of teacher training designed on the basis of a teaching script. In S. Dijkstra, B. Wolters, & P. van der Sijde (Eds.), *Research on instruction design and effects* (pp. 63-78). Englewood Cliffs, NJ: Educational Technology Publications.

Wallberg, H. (1986). Syntheses of research on teaching. In M. C. Wittrock (Ed.), *Handbook of research on teaching* (pp. 214-229). Upper Saddle River, NJ: Merrill/Prentice Hall.

Waller, W. (1932). *The sociology of teaching.* New York: John Wiley and Sons.

Watson, J. B. (1925). *Behaviorism.* New York: Norton.

Weaver, W. T. (1978). Educators in supply and demand: Effects on quality. *School Review, 86*(4), 522-593.

Weaver, W. T. (1979). In search of quality: The need for talent in teaching. *Phi Delta Kappan, 61*(1), 29-33.

Weinstein, C. E., & Mayer, R. E. (1986). The teaching of learning strategies. In M. C. Wittrock (Ed.), *Handbook of research on teaching* (pp. 315-327). New York: Macmillan.

Winebrenner, S. (1992). *Teaching gifted kids in the regular classroom.* Minneapolis, MN: Free Spirit Publishing.

Winebrenner, S. (1996). *Teaching kids with learning difficulties in the regular classroom.* Minneapolis, MN: Free Spirit Publishing.

Wong, H. K., & Wong, R. T. (1998). *How to be an effective teacher: The first days of school.* Mountain View, CA: Harry K. Wong Publications.

Yoshida, M. (1999). *Lesson study: An ethnographic investigation of school-based teacher development in Japan.* Doctoral dissertation, University of Chicago.

Index